I can make
THAT!
IN MY
SLOW
COOKER

Publications International, Ltd.

TABLE OF CONTENTS

SLOW COOKING TIPS

SIZES OF CROCK-POT® SLOW COOKERS

Smaller **CROCK-POT®** slow cookers—such as 1- to 3½-quart models—are the perfect size for cooking for singles, a couple, or empty nesters (and also for serving dips).

While medium-size **CROCK-POT®** slow cookers (those holding somewhere between 3 quarts and 5 quarts) will easily cook enough food at one time to feed a small family. They are also convenient for holiday side dishes or appetizers.

Large **CROCK-POT®** slow cookers are great for large family dinners, holiday entertaining, and potluck suppers. A 6- to 7-quart model is ideal if you like to make meals in advance. Or, have dinner tonight and store leftovers for later.

TYPES OF CROCK-POT® SLOW COOKERS

Current **CROCK-POT®** slow cookers come equipped with many different features and benefits, from auto cook programs to oven-safe stoneware to timed programming. Please visit **WWW.CROCK-POT.COM** to find the **CROCK-POT®** slow cooker that best suits your needs.

How you plan to use a **CROCK-POT®** slow cooker may affect the model you choose to purchase. For everyday cooking, choose a size large enough to serve your family. If you plan to use the **CROCK-POT®** slow cooker primarily for entertaining, choose one of the larger sizes. Basic **CROCK-POT**® slow cookers can hold as little as 16 ounces or as much as 7 quarts. The smallest sizes are great for keeping dips warm on a buffet, while the larger sizes can more readily fit large quantities of food and larger roasts.

COOKING, STIRRING, AND FOOD SAFETY

CROCK-POT® slow cookers are safe to leave unattended. The outer heating base may get hot as it cooks, but it should not pose a fire hazard. The heating element in the heating base functions at a low wattage and is safe for your countertops.

Your **CROCK-POT**® slow cooker should be filled about one-half to three-fourths full for most recipes unless otherwise instructed. Lean meats such as chicken or pork tenderloin will cook faster than meats with more connective tissue and fat such as beef chuck or pork shoulder. Bone-in meats will take longer than boneless cuts. Typical **CROCK-POT**® slow cooker dishes take approximately 7 to 8 hours to reach the simmer point on LOW and about 3 to 4 hours on HIGH. Once the vegetables and meat start to simmer and braise, their flavors will fully blend and meat will become fall-off-the-bone tender.

According to the U.S. Department of Agriculture, all bacteria are killed at a temperature of 165°F. It's important to follow the recommended cooking times and not to open the lid often, especially early in the cooking process when heat is building up inside the unit. If you need to open the lid to check on your food or are adding additional ingredients, remember to allow additional cooking time if necessary to ensure food is cooked through and tender.

Large **CROCK-POT**® slow cookers, the 6- to 7-quart sizes, may benefit from a quick stir halfway through cook time to help distribute heat and promote even cooking. It's usually unnecessary to stir at all, as even ½ cup liquid will help to distribute heat and the stoneware is the perfect medium for holding food at an even temperature throughout the cooking process.

OVEN-SAFE STONEWARE

All **CROCK-POT**® slow cooker removable stoneware inserts may (without their lids) be used safely in ovens at up to 400°F. In addition, all **CROCK-POT**® slow cookers are microwavable without their lids. If you own another slow cooker brand, please refer to your owner's manual for specific stoneware cooking medium tolerances.

FROZEN FOOD

Frozen food can be successfully cooked in a **CROCK-POT**® slow cooker. However, it will require longer cooking

time than the same recipe made with fresh food. It's almost always preferable to thaw frozen food prior to placing it in the **CROCK-POT**® slow cooker. Using an instant-read thermometer is recommended to ensure meat is fully cooked through.

PASTA AND RICE

If you are converting a recipe for a **CROCK-POT**® slow cooker that calls for uncooked pasta, first cook the pasta on the stovetop just until slightly tender. Then add the pasta to the **CROCK-POT**® slow cooker. If you are converting a recipe for the **CROCK-POT**® slow cooker that calls for cooked rice, stir in raw rice with the other recipe ingredients plus ¼ cup extra liquid per ¼ cup of raw rice.

BEANS

Beans must be softened completely before combining with sugar and/or acidic foods in the **CROCK-POT**® slow cooker. Sugar and acid have a hardening effect on beans and will prevent softening. Fully cooked canned beans may be used as a substitute for dried beans.

VEGETABLES

Root vegetables often cook more slowly than meat. Cut vegetables accordingly to cook at the same rate as meat—large or small or lean versus marbled—and place near the sides or bottom of the stoneware to facilitate cooking.

HERBS

Fresh herbs add flavor and color when added at the end of the cooking cycle; if added at the beginning, many fresh herbs' flavor will dissipate over long cook times. Ground and/or dried herbs and spices work well in slow cooking and may be added at the beginning of cook time. For dishes with shorter cook times, hearty fresh herbs such as rosemary and thyme hold up well. The flavor power of all herbs and spices can vary greatly depending on their particular strength and shelf life. Use chili powders and garlic powder sparingly, as these can sometimes intensify over the long cook times. Always taste the finished dish and correct seasonings including salt and pepper.

LIQUIDS

It's not necessary to use more than ½ to 1 cup liquid in most instances since juices in meats and vegetables are retained more in slow cooking than in conventional cooking. Excess liquid can be cooked down and concentrated after slow cooking on the stovetop or by removing meat and vegetables from the stoneware, stirring in one of the following thickeners and setting the **CROCK-POT**® slow cooker to HIGH. Cover; cook on HIGH for approximately 15 minutes or until juices are thickened.

SLOW COOKING TIPS

FLOUR: All-purpose flour is often used to thicken soups or stews. Stir water into the flour in a small bowl until smooth. With the **CROCK-POT**® slow cooker on HIGH, whisk flour mixture into the liquid in the **CROCK-POT**® slow cooker. Cover; cook on HIGH 15 minutes or until the mixture is thickened.

CORNSTARCH: Cornstarch gives sauces a clear, shiny appearance; it's used most often for sweet dessert sauces and stir-fry sauces. Stir water into the cornstarch in a small bowl until the cornstarch is dissolved. Quickly stir this mixture into the liquid in the **CROCK-POT**® slow cooker; the sauce will thicken as soon as the liquid simmers. Cornstarch breaks down with too much heat, so never add it at the beginning of the slow cooking process and turn off the heat as soon as the sauce thickens.

TAPIOCA: Tapioca is a starchy substance extracted from the root of the cassava plant. Its greatest advantage is that it withstands long cooking, making it an ideal choice for slow cooking. Add tapioca at the beginning of cooking and you'll get a clear, thickened sauce in the finished dish. Dishes using tapioca as a thickener are best cooked on the LOW setting; it may become stringy when boiled for a long time.

MILK

Milk, cream, and sour cream break down during extended cooking. When possible, add them during the last 15 to 30 minutes of slow cooking, until just heated through. Condensed soups may be substituted for milk and may cook for extended times.

FISH

Fish is delicate and should be stirred into the **CROCK-POT**® slow cooker gently during the last 15 to 30 minutes of cooking. Cover; cook just until cooked through and serve immediately.

BAKED GOODS

If you wish to prepare bread, cakes, or pudding cakes in a **CROCK-POT**® slow cooker, you may want to purchase a covered, vented metal cake pan accessory for your **CROCK-POT**® slow cooker. You can also use any straight-sided soufflé dish or deep cake pan that will fit into the stoneware of your unit. Baked goods can be prepared directly in the stoneware; however, they can be a little difficult to remove from the insert, so follow the recipe directions carefully.

BREAKFAST AND BRUNCH

OATMEAL WITH MAPLE-GLAZED APPLES AND CRANBERRIES

3 cups water

2 cups quick-cooking or old-fashioned oats

¼ teaspoon salt

1 teaspoon unsalted butter

2 medium red or Golden Delicious apples, unpeeled and cut into ½-inch pieces

¼ teaspoon ground cinnamon

2 tablespoons maple syrup

4 tablespoons dried cranberries

1. Combine water, oats and salt in **CROCK-POT®** slow cooker. Cover; cook on LOW 8 hours.

2. Melt butter in large nonstick skillet over medium heat. Add apples and cinnamon; cook and stir 4 to 5 minutes or until tender. Stir in syrup; heat through.

3. Serve oatmeal with apple mixture and cranberries.

Makes 4 servings

BLUEBERRY-ORANGE
FRENCH TOAST CASSEROLE

½ cup sugar

½ cup milk

2 eggs

4 egg whites

1 tablespoon grated orange peel

½ teaspoon vanilla

6 slices whole wheat bread, cut into 1-inch cubes

1 cup fresh blueberries

Maple syrup (optional)

1. Coat inside of **CROCK-POT**® slow cooker with nonstick cooking spray.

2. Stir sugar and milk in medium bowl until sugar dissolves. Whisk in eggs, egg whites, orange peel and vanilla. Add bread and blueberries; stir to coat. Remove mixture to **CROCK-POT**® slow cooker.

3. Cover; cook on LOW 3 to 4 hours or on HIGH 1½ to 2 hours or until toothpick inserted into center comes out clean. Turn off heat. Let stand 5 minutes before serving. Serve with syrup, if desired.

Makes 6 servings

WAKE-UP POTATO AND SAUSAGE BREAKFAST CASSEROLE

1 pound kielbasa or smoked sausage, diced

1 cup chopped onion

1 cup chopped red bell pepper

1 package (20 ounces) refrigerated Southwestern-style hash browns*

10 eggs

1 cup milk

1 cup (4 ounces) shredded Monterey Jack or sharp Cheddar cheese

*You may substitute O'Brien potatoes and add ½ teaspoon chile pepper.

1. Coat inside of **CROCK-POT**® slow cooker with nonstick cooking spray. Heat large skillet over medium-high heat. Add sausage and onion; cook and stir 6 to 8 minutes or until sausage is browned. Drain fat. Stir in bell pepper.

2. Place one third of potatoes in **CROCK-POT**® slow cooker. Top with half of sausage mixture. Repeat layers. Spread remaining one third of potatoes evenly on top.

3. Whisk eggs and milk in medium bowl. Pour evenly over potatoes. Cover; cook on LOW 6 to 7 hours.

4. Turn off heat. Sprinkle cheese over casserole; let stand 10 minutes or until cheese is melted.

Makes 8 servings

TIP To remove casserole from **CROCK-POT**® slow cooker, omit step 4. Run a rubber spatula around the edge of casserole, lifting the bottom slightly. Invert onto a large plate. Place a large serving plate on top; invert again. Sprinkle with cheese and let stand until cheese is melted. Cut into wedges.

BANANA NUT BREAD

⅓ cup butter	1¾ cups all-purpose flour
3 mashed bananas	2 teaspoons baking powder
⅔ cup sugar	½ teaspoon salt
2 eggs, beaten	¼ teaspoon baking soda
2 tablespoons dark corn syrup	½ cup chopped walnuts

1. Grease and flour inside of **CROCK-POT**® slow cooker. Beat butter in large bowl with electric mixer at medium speed until fluffy. Gradually beat in bananas, sugar, eggs and corn syrup until smooth.

2. Combine flour, baking powder, salt and baking soda in small bowl; stir to blend. Beat flour mixture into banana mixture. Add walnuts; mix thoroughly. Pour batter into **CROCK-POT**® slow cooker.

3. Cover; cook on HIGH 2 to 3 hours. Cool completely; turn bread out onto large serving platter.

Makes 1 loaf

TIP Banana Nut Bread freezes well for future use.

ORANGE SOUFFLÉ

6 tablespoons unsalted butter, softened and divided

1¼ cups sugar, divided

Grated peel of 1 orange

½ cup milk

6 tablespoons all-purpose flour

8 egg yolks

6 tablespoons orange-flavored liqueur

1 tablespoon vanilla extract

10 egg whites

1 teaspoon salt

Whipping cream

Fresh raspberries

Sprigs fresh mint (optional)

1. Butter inside of **CROCK-POT**® slow cooker with 2 tablespoons butter. Pour in ⅓ cup sugar; turn to evenly coat bottom and sides of **CROCK-POT**® slow cooker.

2. Place ⅔ cup sugar and orange peel in food processor or blender; process until orange peel is evenly ground and well combined.

3. Whisk orange sugar, milk and flour in medium saucepan; cook and stir over medium heat until just beginning to thicken. Bring to a boil over high heat; cook and stir 30 seconds. Remove from heat. Let mixture cool slightly; beat in egg yolks, one at a time. Add orange liqueur, remaining 4 tablespoons butter and vanilla to egg yolk mixture; let stand at room temperature 20 minutes to cool.

4. Beat egg whites in clean, dry bowl until foamy. Add salt; beat to soft peaks. Sprinkle in remaining ¼ cup sugar; beat to stiff peaks. Fold one quarter of beaten egg whites into cooled batter. Fold in remaining egg whites; gently remove to **CROCK-POT**® slow cooker. Cover; cook on HIGH 1 hour or until soufflé is fully set. Top with whipped cream and raspberries. Garnish with mint.

Makes 10 servings

HASH BROWN AND SAUSAGE BREAKFAST CASSEROLE

4 cups frozen southern-style hash browns

3 tablespoons unsalted butter

1 large onion, chopped

8 ounces (about 2 cups) sliced mushrooms

3 cloves garlic, minced

2 precooked apple chicken sausages, cut into 1-inch slices

1 package (10 ounces) frozen chopped spinach, thawed and squeezed dry

8 eggs

1 cup milk

1 teaspoon salt

¼ teaspoon black pepper

1½ cups (6 ounces) shredded sharp Cheddar cheese, divided

1. Coat inside of **CROCK-POT**® slow cooker with nonstick cooking spray. Place hash browns in **CROCK-POT**® slow cooker.

2. Melt butter in large nonstick skillet over medium-high heat. Add onion, mushrooms and garlic; cook 4 to 5 minutes or until onion is just starting to brown, stirring occasionally. Stir in sausage slices; cook 2 minutes. Add spinach; cook 2 minutes or until mushrooms are tender. Stir sausage mixture into **CROCK-POT**® slow cooker with hash browns until combined.

3. Combine eggs, milk, salt and pepper in large bowl; whisk until blended. Pour over hash brown mixture in **CROCK-POT**® slow cooker. Top with 1 cup cheese. Cover; cook on LOW 4 to 4½ hours or on HIGH 1½ to 2 hours or until eggs are set. Top with remaining ½ cup cheese. Cut into wedges to serve.

Makes 6 to 8 servings

BREAKFAST BERRY BREAD PUDDING

6 cups bread, preferably sourdough, cut into ¾- to 1-inch cubes

1 cup raisins

½ cup slivered almonds, toasted*

6 eggs, beaten

1¾ cups milk

1½ cups packed brown sugar

1½ teaspoons ground cinnamon

1 teaspoon vanilla

3 cups sliced fresh strawberries

2 cups fresh blueberries

*To toast almonds, spread in single layer in heavy skillet. Cook and stir over medium heat 1 to 2 minutes or until nuts are lightly browned.

1. Coat inside of **CROCK-POT**® slow cooker with nonstick cooking spray. Add bread, raisins and almonds; toss to combine.

2. Whisk eggs, milk, brown sugar, cinnamon and vanilla in large bowl. Pour egg mixture over bread mixture; stir to coat. Cover; cook on LOW 4 to 4½ hours or on HIGH 3 hours.

3. Remove stoneware from **CROCK-POT**® slow cooker. Let stand until set. Serve with berries.

Makes 12 servings

ORANGE CRANBERRY NUT BREAD

2 cups all-purpose flour	2 teaspoons dried orange peel
½ cup chopped pecans	⅔ cup boiling water
1 teaspoon baking powder	¾ cup sugar
½ teaspoon baking soda	2 tablespoons shortening
¼ teaspoon salt	1 egg, lightly beaten
1 cup dried cranberries	1 teaspoon vanilla

1. Coat inside of 3-quart **CROCK-POT®** slow cooker with nonstick cooking spray. Combine flour, pecans, baking powder, baking soda and salt in medium bowl; stir to blend.

2. Combine cranberries and orange peel in another medium bowl; stir in boiling water. Add sugar, shortening, egg and vanilla; stir just until blended. Add flour mixture; stir just until blended.

3. Pour batter into **CROCK-POT®** slow cooker. Cover; cook on HIGH 1 to 1½ hours or until edges begin to brown and toothpick inserted into center comes out clean.

4. Remove stoneware from **CROCK-POT®** slow cooker. Cool on wire rack 10 minutes. Remove bread from insert; cool completely on rack.

Makes 8 to 10 servings

TIP This recipe works best in round **CROCK-POT®** slow cookers.

ROASTED PEPPER AND SOURDOUGH EGG DISH

3 cups sourdough bread cubes

1 jar (12 ounces) roasted red pepper strips, drained

1 cup (4 ounces) shredded Monterey Jack cheese

1 cup (4 ounces) shredded sharp Cheddar cheese

1 cup cottage cheese

6 eggs

1 cup milk

¼ cup chopped fresh cilantro

¼ teaspoon black pepper

1. Coat inside of **CROCK-POT®** slow cooker with nonstick cooking spray. Add bread. Arrange roasted peppers evenly over bread cubes; sprinkle with Monterey Jack and Cheddar cheeses.

2. Place cottage cheese in food processor or blender; process until smooth. Add eggs and milk; process just until blended. Stir in cilantro and black pepper.

3. Pour egg mixture into **CROCK-POT®** slow cooker. Cover; cook on LOW 3 to 3½ hours or on HIGH 2 to 2½ hours or until eggs are firm but still moist.

Makes 6 servings

MAPLE, BACON AND RASPBERRY PANCAKE

5 slices bacon

2 cups pancake mix

1 cup water

½ cup maple syrup, plus additional for serving

1 cup fresh raspberries

3 tablespoons chopped pecans, toasted*

*To toast pecans, spread in single layer in heavy skillet. Cook and stir over medium heat 1 to 2 minutes or until nuts are lightly browned.

1. Heat large skillet over medium heat. Add bacon; cook and stir until crisp. Remove to paper towel-lined plate using slotted spoon; crumble.

2. Brush inside of 5-quart **CROCK-POT**® slow cooker with 1 to 2 tablespoons bacon fat from skillet. Combine pancake mix, water and ½ cup syrup in large bowl; stir to blend. Pour half of batter into **CROCK-POT**® slow cooker; top with half of raspberries, half of bacon and half of pecans. Pour remaining half of batter over top; sprinkle with remaining raspberries, bacon and pecans.

3. Cover; cook on HIGH 1½ to 2 hours or until pancake has risen and is cooked through. Turn off heat. Let stand, uncovered, 10 to 15 minutes. Remove pancake from **CROCK-POT**® slow cooker; cut into eight pieces. Serve with additional syrup.

Makes 8 servings

BROCCOLI AND CHEESE STRATA

2 cups chopped broccoli

4 slices firm white bread (½ inch thick)

4 teaspoons butter

1½ cups (6 ounces) shredded Cheddar cheese

1½ cups milk

3 eggs

½ teaspoon salt

½ teaspoon hot pepper sauce

⅛ teaspoon black pepper

1 cup water

1. Spray 1-quart casserole or soufflé dish that fits inside of **CROCK-POT®** slow cooker with nonstick cooking spray. Bring 4 cups water to a boil in large saucepan; cook broccoli 10 minutes or until tender. Drain.

2. Spread one side of each bread slice with 1 teaspoon butter. Arrange 2 slices bread, buttered sides up, in prepared casserole. Layer cheese, broccoli and remaining 2 bread slices, buttered sides down.

3. Whisk milk, eggs, salt, hot pepper sauce and black pepper in medium bowl; slowly pour over bread.

4. Place small wire rack in **CROCK-POT®** slow cooker. Pour in 1 cup water. Place casserole on rack. Cover; cook on HIGH 3 hours.

Makes 4 servings

RAISIN-OAT QUICK BREAD

1½ cups all-purpose flour, plus additional for dusting

⅔ cup old-fashioned oats

⅓ cup milk

4 teaspoons baking powder

1 teaspoon ground cinnamon

½ teaspoon salt

½ cup packed raisins

1 cup sugar

2 eggs, slightly beaten

½ cup (1 stick) unsalted butter, melted, plus additional for serving

1 teaspoon vanilla

1. Spray inside of ovenproof glass or ceramic loaf pan that fits inside of **CROCK-POT**® slow cooker with nonstick cooking spray; dust with flour.

2. Combine oats and milk in small bowl; let stand 10 minutes.

3. Meanwhile, combine 1½ cups flour, baking powder, cinnamon and salt in large bowl; stir in raisins. Whisk sugar, eggs, ½ cup melted butter and vanilla in separate medium bowl; stir in oat mixture. Pour sugar mixture into flour mixture; stir just until moistened. Pour into prepared pan. Place in **CROCK-POT**® slow cooker. Cover; cook on HIGH 2½ to 3 hours or until toothpick inserted into center comes out clean.

4. Remove bread from **CROCK-POT**® slow cooker; let cool in pan 10 minutes. Remove bread from pan; let cool on wire rack 3 minutes before slicing. Serve with additional butter, if desired.

Makes 12 servings

OATMEAL CRÈME BRÛLÉE

4 cups boiling water

3 cups quick-cooking oatmeal

½ teaspoon salt

6 egg yolks

½ cup granulated sugar

2 cups whipping cream

1 teaspoon vanilla

¼ cup packed light brown sugar

Fresh berries (optional)

1. Coat inside of **CROCK-POT**® slow cooker with nonstick cooking spray. Pour water into **CROCK-POT**® slow cooker. Stir in oatmeal and salt; cover.

2. Combine egg yolks and granulated sugar in medium bowl; stir to blend. Heat cream and vanilla in medium saucepan over medium heat until small bubbles begin to form at edge of pan. *Do not boil.* Remove from heat. Whisking constantly, pour ½ cup hot cream into egg yolk mixture in thin stream. Whisk egg mixture back into cream in saucepan, stirring rapidly to blend well. Spoon mixture over oatmeal. *Do not stir.*

3. Turn **CROCK-POT**® slow cooker to LOW. Line lid with two paper towels. Cover; cook on LOW 3 to 3½ hours or until custard is set.

4. Sprinkle brown sugar over surface of custard. Line lid with two new dry paper towels. Cover tightly; cook on LOW 10 to 15 minutes or until brown sugar melts. Serve with fresh berries, if desired.

Makes 4 to 6 servings

BLUEBERRY-BANANA PANCAKES

2 cups all-purpose flour

⅓ cup sugar

1 tablespoon baking powder

½ teaspoon baking soda

½ teaspoon salt

½ teaspoon ground cinnamon

1¾ cups milk

2 eggs, lightly beaten

¼ cup (½ stick) unsalted butter, melted

1 teaspoon vanilla

1 cup fresh blueberries

2 small bananas, sliced

Maple syrup

1. Combine flour, sugar, baking powder, baking soda, salt and cinnamon in large bowl; stir to blend. Combine milk, eggs, butter and vanilla in separate medium bowl; stir to blend. Pour milk mixture into flour mixture; stir until moistened. Fold in blueberries until blended.

2. Coat inside of **CROCK-POT**® slow cooker with nonstick cooking spray. Pour batter into **CROCK-POT**® slow cooker. Cover; cook on HIGH 2 hours or until puffed and toothpick inserted into center comes out clean. Cut into wedges; top with bananas and syrup.

Makes 4 to 6 servings

SIMMERING SIPS

TRIPLE DELICIOUS HOT CHOCOLATE

3 cups milk, divided

⅓ cup sugar

¼ cup unsweetened cocoa powder

¼ teaspoon salt

¾ teaspoon vanilla

1 cup whipping cream

1 square (1 ounce) bittersweet chocolate, chopped

1 square (1 ounce) white chocolate, chopped

Whipped cream

6 teaspoons mini semisweet chocolate chips or shaved bittersweet chocolate

1. Combine ½ cup milk, sugar, cocoa and salt in **CROCK-POT**® slow cooker; whisk until smooth. Stir in remaining 2½ cups milk and vanilla. Cover; cook on LOW 2 hours.

2. Stir in cream. Cover; cook on LOW 10 minutes. Stir in bittersweet and white chocolate until melted.

3. Pour hot chocolate into mugs. Top each serving evenly with whipped cream and chocolate chips.

Makes 6 servings

HOT MULLED CIDER

½ gallon apple cider

½ cup packed brown sugar

1½ teaspoons balsamic or cider vinegar (optional)

1 teaspoon vanilla

1 whole cinnamon stick

6 whole cloves

½ cup applejack or bourbon (optional)

1. Combine cider, brown sugar, vinegar, if desired, vanilla, cinnamon stick and cloves in **CROCK-POT®** slow cooker; stir to blend. Cover; cook on LOW 5 to 6 hours.

2. Remove and discard cinnamon stick and cloves. Stir in applejack just before serving, if desired. Serve warm in mugs.

Makes 16 servings

VIENNESE COFFEE

3 cups strong freshly brewed hot coffee

3 tablespoons chocolate syrup

1 teaspoon sugar

⅓ cup whipping cream, plus additional for topping

¼ cup crème de cacao or Irish cream

Chocolate shavings (optional)

1. Combine coffee, chocolate syrup and sugar in **CROCK-POT**® slow cooker. Cover; cook on LOW 2 to 2½ hours.

2. Stir ⅓ cup whipping cream and crème de cacao into **CROCK-POT**® slow cooker. Cover; cook on LOW 30 minutes or until heated through. Ladle coffee into coffee mugs. Top with additional whipped cream and chocolate shavings, if desired.

Makes 4 servings

CHAI TEA CHERRIES 'N' CREAM

2 cans (15½ ounces *each*) pitted cherries in pear juice

2 cups water

½ cup orange juice

1 cup sugar

4 cardamom pods

2 whole cinnamon sticks, broken in half

1 teaspoon grated orange peel

¼ ounce coarsely chopped candied ginger

4 whole cloves

2 whole black peppercorns

4 green tea bags

1 container (6 ounces) black cherry yogurt

1 quart vanilla ice cream

Sprigs fresh mint (optional)

1. Drain cherries, reserving juice. Combine reserved pear juice, water and orange juice in **CROCK-POT®** slow cooker. Mix in sugar, cardamom pods, cinnamon sticks, orange peel, ginger, cloves and peppercorns. Cover; cook on HIGH 1½ hours.

2. Remove spices with slotted spoon; discard. Stir in tea bags and reserved cherries. Cover; cook on HIGH 30 minutes.

3. Turn off heat. Remove and discard tea bags. Remove cherries from liquid; set aside. Let liquid cool until just warm. Whisk in yogurt until smooth.

4. To serve, divide warm cherries and yogurt sauce among wine or cocktail glasses. Top each serving with ice cream; swirl lightly. Garnish with mint.

Makes 8 servings

CINNAMON LATTÉ

6 cups double-strength
   brewed coffee*

2 cups half-and-half

1 cup sugar

1 teaspoon vanilla

3 whole cinnamon sticks,
   plus additional for
   garnish

   Whipped cream
   (optional)

*Double the amount of coffee grounds normally
used to brew coffee. Or substitute 8 teaspoons
instant coffee dissolved in 6 cups boiling water.

1. Blend coffee, half-and-half,
sugar and vanilla in 3- to 4-quart
CROCK-POT® slow cooker. Add
3 cinnamon sticks. Cover; cook
on HIGH 3 hours.

2. Remove and discard
cinnamon sticks. Garnish with
additional cinnamon sticks and
whipped cream.

Makes 6 to 8 servings

GINGER PEAR CIDER

8 cups pear juice or cider

¾ cup lemon juice

¼ to ½ cup honey

10 whole cloves

2 whole cinnamon sticks, plus additional for garnish

8 slices fresh ginger

1. Combine pear juice, lemon juice, honey, cloves, 2 cinnamon sticks and ginger in 5-quart **CROCK-POT**® slow cooker.

2. Cover; cook on LOW 5 to 6 hours or on HIGH 2½ to 3 hours. Remove and discard cloves, cinnamon sticks and ginger before serving. Garnish with additional cinnamon sticks.

Makes 8 to 10 servings

WARM AND SPICY FRUIT PUNCH

4 whole cinnamon sticks

1 orange

1 8-inch square double-thickness cheesecloth

1 teaspoon whole allspice

½ teaspoon whole cloves

7 cups water

1 can (12 ounces) frozen cran-raspberry juice concentrate, thawed

1 can (6 ounces) frozen lemonade concentrate, thawed

2 cans (5½ ounces *each*) apricot nectar

1. Break cinnamon sticks into pieces. Remove strips of orange peel with vegetable peeler or paring knife. Squeeze juice from orange; set juice aside.

2. Rinse cheesecloth; squeeze out water. Wrap cinnamon sticks, orange peel, allspice and cloves in cheesecloth. Tie bag securely with cotton string or strip of cheesecloth.

3. Combine reserved orange juice, water, juice concentrates and apricot nectar in **CROCK-POT®** slow cooker; add spice bag. Cover; cook on LOW 5 to 6 hours. Remove and discard spice bag before serving.

Makes about 14 servings

TIP To keep punch warm during a party, place your **CROCK-POT®** slow cooker on the buffet table and turn the setting to LOW or WARM.

MULLED APPLE CIDER

2 quarts bottled apple cider or juice (not unfiltered)

¼ cup packed light brown sugar

1 (8-inch) square double-thickness cheesecloth

8 whole allspice berries

4 whole cinnamon sticks, broken in half, plus additional for serving

12 whole cloves

1 large orange

1. Combine apple cider and brown sugar in **CROCK-POT®** slow cooker.

2. Rinse cheesecloth; squeeze out water. Wrap allspice berries and cinnamon stick halves in cheesecloth; tie securely with cotton string or strip of cheesecloth.

3. Stick cloves randomly into orange; cut orange into quarters. Place spice bag and orange quarters in cider mixture. Cover; cook on HIGH 2½ to 3 hours.

4. Remove and discard spice bag and orange quarters before serving. Ladle cider into mugs. Garnish with additional cinnamon sticks. Turn **CROCK-POT®** slow cooker to LOW to keep cider warm up to 3 hours.

Makes 10 servings

TIP To make inserting cloves into the orange a little easier, first pierce the orange skin with the point of a wooden skewer. Remove the skewer and insert a clove.

SIMMERING SIPS

HOT TROPICS SIPPER

4 cups pineapple juice

2 cups apple juice

1 container (about 11 ounces) apricot nectar

½ cup packed dark brown sugar

1 medium orange, thinly sliced plus additional for garnish

1 medium lemon, thinly sliced plus additional for garnish

3 whole cinnamon sticks

6 whole cloves

1. Combine pineapple juice, apple juice, nectar, brown sugar, orange slices, lemon slices, cinnamon sticks and cloves in **CROCK-POT®** slow cooker. Cover; cook on HIGH 3½ to 4 hours.

2. Strain immediately (beverage will turn bitter if fruit and spices remain after cooking is complete). Remove and discard cinnamon sticks. Serve with additional orange and lemon slices, if desired.

Makes 8 servings

MINTED HOT COCOA

6 cups milk

¾ cup semisweet chocolate pieces

½ cup sugar

½ cup unsweetened cocoa powder

1 teaspoon vanilla

½ teaspoon mint extract

10 sprigs fresh mint, tied together with kitchen string, plus additional for garnish

Whipped cream (optional)

1. Combine milk, chocolate, sugar, cocoa, vanilla and mint extract in **CROCK-POT®** slow cooker; stir to blend. Add 10 mint sprigs. Cover; cook on LOW 3 to 4 hours.

2. Uncover; remove and discard mint sprigs. Whisk cocoa mixture well. Cover until ready to serve. Garnish each serving with whipped cream and additional mint sprigs.

Makes 6 to 8 servings

MULLED CRANBERRY TEA

2 tea bags

1 cup boiling water

1 bottle (48 ounces) cranberry juice

½ cup dried cranberries (optional)

⅓ cup sugar

1 lemon, cut into ¼-inch slices

4 whole cinnamon sticks plus additional for garnish

6 whole cloves

Thin lemon slices (optional)

1. Place tea bags in **CROCK-POT**® slow cooker. Pour boiling water over tea bags; cover and let steep 5 minutes. Remove and discard tea bags.

2. Stir in cranberry juice, cranberries, if desired, sugar, 1 sliced lemon, 4 cinnamon sticks and cloves. Cover; cook on LOW 2 to 3 hours or on HIGH 1 to 2 hours.

3. Remove and discard cooked lemon slices, cinnamon sticks and cloves. Serve in warm mugs with additional cinnamon sticks or fresh lemon slices, if desired.

Makes 8 servings

TIP The flavor and aroma of crushed or ground herbs and spices may lessen during long cooking time. So, for slow cooking in your **CROCK-POT**® slow cooker, you may use whole herbs and spices. Just be sure to taste and adjust seasonings before serving.

GINGER-LIME MARTINI

2 cups sugar

1 cup water

1 (5-inch) piece fresh ginger, peeled and thinly sliced

3 cups vodka, chilled

2 cups lime juice

Crushed ice

Green olives (optional)

1. Place sugar, water and ginger in **CROCK-POT®** slow cooker. Cover; cook on LOW 6 to 8 hours or on HIGH 3 to 4 hours.

2. Strain ginger syrup; cool. Refrigerate in airtight container until needed, up to 7 days.

3. For each serving, combine 2 ounces ginger syrup, 3 ounces vodka and 2 ounces lime juice in martini shaker half filled with crushed ice. Shake to combine; strain into chilled martini glass. Garnish with olives.

Makes 8 servings

HOMEMADE GINGER ALE: Pour ½ cup chilled ginger syrup over ice in 16-ounce glass. Top off with 1 cup soda water and stir gently to combine.

WARM HONEY LEMONADE

4½ cups water

2½ cups lemon juice

1 cup orange juice

1 cup honey

¼ cup sugar

Lemon slices (optional)

1. Combine water, lemon juice, orange juice, honey and sugar in **CROCK-POT®** slow cooker; whisk well.

2. Cover; cook on LOW 2 hours. Whisk well before serving. Garnish with lemon slices.

Makes 9 servings

SPICED APPLE TEA

- 3 bags cinnamon herbal tea
- 3 cups boiling water
- 2 cups unsweetened apple juice
- 6 whole cloves
- 1 whole cinnamon stick

1. Place tea bags in **CROCK-POT**® slow cooker. Pour boiling water over tea bags; cover and let steep 10 minutes. Remove and discard tea bags.

2. Add apple juice, cloves and cinnamon stick to **CROCK-POT**® slow cooker. Cover; cook on LOW 2 to 3 hours. Remove and discard cloves and cinnamon stick. Serve warm in mugs.

Makes 4 servings

MOCHA SUPREME

2 quarts strong brewed coffee

½ cup instant hot chocolate beverage mix

1 whole cinnamon stick, broken in half

1 cup whipping cream

1 tablespoon powdered sugar

1. Place coffee, hot chocolate mix and cinnamon stick halves in **CROCK-POT®** slow cooker; stir to blend. Cover; cook on HIGH 2 to 2½ hours. Remove and discard cinnamon stick halves.

2. Beat cream in medium bowl with electric mixer on high speed until soft peaks form. Add powdered sugar; beat until stiff peaks form. Ladle mocha mixture into mugs; top with whipped cream.

Makes 8 servings

TIP To whip cream quickly, chill the beaters and bowl in the freezer 15 minutes.

MULLED CRAN-APPLE PUNCH

1 orange	3 whole cinnamon sticks, plus additional for garnish
1 lemon	1 (5-inch) square double-thickness cheesecloth
1 lime	
15 whole black peppercorns	6 cups apple juice
10 whole cloves	3 cups cranberry juice
10 whole allspice	3 tablespoons maple syrup

1. Use vegetable peeler to remove 5 to 6 (2- to 3-inch-long) sections of orange, lemon and lime peel, being careful to avoid white pith. Squeeze juice from orange; set juice aside.

2. Place peels, peppercorns, cloves, allspice and 3 cinnamon sticks in center of cheesecloth. Bring corners together; tie with cotton string or strip of additional cheesecloth.

3. Pour apple juice, cranberry juice, maple syrup and reserved orange juice into 5-quart **CROCK-POT**® slow cooker; add spice bag. Cover; cook on LOW 5 to 6 hours or on HIGH 2½ to 3 hours. Garnish with additional cinnamon sticks.

Makes 8 servings

INFUSED MINT MOJITO

2 cups water

2 cups sugar

2 bunches fresh mint, stems removed, plus additional for garnish

¾ to 1 cup fresh-squeezed lime juice

1 bottle (750 mL) light rum

2 liters club soda

Fresh lime slices (optional)

1. Combine water, sugar and mint in **CROCK-POT®** slow cooker; stir to blend. Cover; cook on HIGH 3½ hours.

2. Strain into large pitcher. Stir in lime juice and rum. Cover and refrigerate until cold.

3. To serve, fill tall glasses halfway with fresh ice. Pour ¾ cup mint syrup over ice; top off with club soda to taste. Garnish with additional fresh mint leaves and lime slices.

Makes 10 to 12 servings

MUCHO MOCHA COCOA

4 cups whole milk

4 cups half-and-half

1 cup chocolate syrup

⅓ cup instant coffee granules

2 tablespoons sugar

2 whole cinnamon sticks

1. Combine milk, half-and-half, chocolate syrup, coffee granules, sugar and cinnamon sticks in **CROCK-POT**® slow cooker; stir to blend. Cover; cook on LOW 3 hours.

2. Remove and discard cinnamon sticks. Serve warm in mugs.

Makes 9 servings

TIP This is great for a party. If desired, add 1 ounce of rum or whiskey to each serving.

SIMMERING SIPS

CHAI TEA

2 quarts (8 cups) water

8 bags black tea

¾ cup sugar*

8 slices fresh ginger

5 whole cinnamon sticks, plus additional for garnish

16 whole cloves

16 whole cardamom seeds, pods removed (optional)

1 cup milk

*Chai tea is typically sweet. For less-sweet tea, reduce sugar to ½ cup.

1. Combine water, tea bags, sugar, ginger, 5 cinnamon sticks, cloves and cardamom, if desired, in **CROCK-POT**® slow cooker; stir to blend. Cover; cook on HIGH 2 to 2½ hours.

2. Strain mixture; discard solids. (At this point, tea may be covered and refrigerated up to 3 days.)

3. Stir in milk just before serving. Garnish with additional cinnamon sticks.

Makes 8 to 10 servings

CRAZY CASSEROLES

TUNA CASSEROLE

2 cans (10¾ ounces *each*) cream of celery soup

2 cans (5 ounces *each*) tuna in water, drained and flaked

1 cup water

2 carrots, chopped

1 small red onion, chopped

¼ teaspoon black pepper

1 raw egg, uncracked

8 ounces hot cooked egg noodles
Plain dry bread crumbs

2 tablespoons chopped fresh Italian parsley

1. Stir soup, tuna, water, carrots, onion and pepper into **CROCK-POT®** slow cooker. Place whole unpeeled egg on top. Cover; cook on LOW 4 to 5 hours or on HIGH 1½ to 3 hours.

2. Remove egg; stir in pasta. Cover; cook on HIGH 30 to 60 minutes or until onion is tender. Meanwhile, mash egg in small bowl; mix in bread crumbs and parsley. Top casserole with bread crumb mixture.

Makes 6 servings

NOTE: This casserole calls for a raw egg. The egg will hard-cook in its shell in the **CROCK-POT®** slow cooker.

WILD RICE AND MUSHROOM CASSEROLE

2 tablespoons olive oil

½ medium red onion, finely diced

1 green bell pepper, finely diced

8 ounces button mushrooms, thinly sliced

2 cloves garlic, minced

1 can (14 ounces) diced tomatoes, drained

1 teaspoon dried oregano

1 teaspoon paprika

2 tablespoons butter

2 tablespoons all-purpose flour

1½ cups milk

2 cups (8 ounces) shredded pepper jack, Cheddar or Swiss cheese

1 teaspoon salt

½ teaspoon black pepper

2 cups wild rice, cooked according to package instructions

1. Heat oil in large skillet over medium heat. Add onion, bell pepper and mushrooms; cook 5 to 6 minutes, stirring occasionally, until vegetables soften. Add garlic, tomatoes, oregano and paprika; cook until heated through. Remove to large bowl to cool.

2. Melt butter in same skillet over medium heat; whisk in flour. Cook and stir 4 to 5 minutes or until smooth and golden. Whisk in milk and bring to a boil. Whisk in cheese. Season with salt and black pepper.

3. Combine wild rice with vegetables in large bowl. Fold in cheese sauce; mix gently.

4. Coat inside of **CROCK-POT**® slow cooker with nonstick cooking spray. Pour wild rice mixture into **CROCK-POT**® slow cooker. Cover; cook on LOW 4 to 6 hours or on HIGH 2 to 3 hours.

Makes 4 to 6 servings

JAMAICA-ME-CRAZY CHICKEN TROPICALE

2 sweet potatoes, cut into 2-inch pieces

1 can (20 ounces) pineapple tidbits in pineapple juice, drained and juice reserved

1 can (8 ounces) water chestnuts, drained and sliced

1 cup golden raisins

4 boneless, skinless chicken breasts

4 teaspoons Caribbean jerk seasoning

¼ cup dried onion flakes

3 tablespoons grated fresh ginger

2 tablespoons Worcestershire sauce

1 tablespoon grated lime peel

1 teaspoon whole cumin seeds, slightly crushed

Hot cooked rice (optional)

1. Combine potatoes, pineapple, water chestnuts and raisins in **CROCK-POT®** slow cooker; stir to blend. Sprinkle chicken with seasoning. Place chicken on top of sweet potato mixture.

2. Combine reserved pineapple juice, onion flakes, ginger, Worcestershire sauce, lime peel and cumin seeds in small bowl; pour over chicken. Cover; cook on LOW 7 to 9 hours or on HIGH 3 to 4 hours or until chicken and potatoes are fork-tender. Serve with rice, if desired.

Makes 4 servings

RAVIOLI CASSEROLE

8 ounces pork or turkey Italian sausage, casings removed

½ cup minced onion

1½ cups marinara sauce

1 can (about 14 ounces) Italian-style diced tomatoes

2 packages (9 ounces *each*) refrigerated meatless ravioli, such as wild mushroom or three cheese, divided

1½ cups (6 ounces) shredded mozzarella cheese, divided

Chopped fresh Italian parsley (optional)

1. Heat large skillet over medium-high heat. Brown sausage and onion 6 to 8 minutes, stirring to break up meat. Drain fat. Stir in marinara sauce and tomatoes; mix well. Remove from heat.

2. Coat inside of **CROCK-POT®** slow cooker with nonstick cooking spray. Spoon 1 cup sauce into **CROCK-POT®** slow cooker. Layer half of 1 package of ravioli over sauce; top with additional ½ cup sauce. Repeat layering once; top with ½ cup cheese. Repeat layering with remaining package ravioli and all remaining sauce, reserve remaining ½ cup cheese. Cover; cook on LOW 2½ to 3 hours or on HIGH 1½ to 2 hours or until sauce is heated through and ravioli is tender.

3. Sprinkle remaining ½ cup cheese over top of casserole. Cover; cook on HIGH 15 minutes or until cheese is melted. Garnish with parsley.

Makes 4 to 6 servings

CORNBREAD AND BEAN CASSEROLE

1 medium onion, chopped

1 medium green bell pepper, diced

2 cloves garlic, minced

1 can (about 15 ounces) red kidney beans, rinsed and drained

1 can (about 15 ounces) pinto beans, rinsed and drained

1 can (about 15 ounces) diced tomatoes with mild green chiles

1 can (8 ounces) tomato sauce

1 teaspoon chili powder

½ teaspoon ground cumin

½ teaspoon black pepper

¼ teaspoon hot pepper sauce

1 cup yellow cornmeal

1 cup all-purpose flour

2½ teaspoons baking powder

1 tablespoon sugar

½ teaspoon salt

1¼ cups milk

2 eggs

3 tablespoons vegetable oil

1 can (8½ ounces) cream-style corn

1. Coat inside of **CROCK-POT**® slow cooker with nonstick cooking spray. Heat large skillet over medium heat. Add onion, bell pepper and garlic; cook and stir 5 minutes or until tender. Remove to **CROCK-POT**® slow cooker.

2. Stir beans, diced tomatoes, tomato sauce, chili powder, cumin, black pepper and hot pepper sauce into **CROCK-POT**® slow cooker. Cover; cook on HIGH 1 hour.

3. Combine cornmeal, flour, baking powder, sugar and salt in large bowl. Stir in milk, eggs and oil; mix well. Stir in corn. Spoon evenly over bean mixture in **CROCK-POT**® slow cooker. Cover; cook on HIGH 1½ to 2 hours or until cornbread topping is golden brown.

Makes 8 servings

TIP Spoon any remaining cornbread topping into greased muffin cups. Bake 30 minutes at 375°F or until golden brown.

FALL BEEF AND BEER CASSEROLE

2 tablespoons oil

1½ pounds cubed beef stew meat

2 tablespoons all-purpose flour

1 cup beef broth

2 cups brown ale or beer

1 cup water

1 onion, sliced

2 carrots, sliced

1 leek, sliced

2 stalks celery, sliced

1 cup mushrooms, sliced

1 turnip, peeled and cubed

1 teaspoon mixed fresh herbs

1. Heat oil in large skillet over medium-high heat. Add beef; cook and stir 6 to 8 minutes until browned on all sides. Remove to **CROCK-POT**® slow cooker.

2. Sprinkle flour over contents of skillet; cook and stir 2 minutes. Gradually stir in broth, ale and water. Bring to a boil; pour over beef.

3. Add onion, carrots, leek, celery, mushrooms, turnip and herbs to **CROCK-POT**® slow cooker; stir to blend. Cover; cook on LOW 8 to 10 hours or on HIGH 4 to 6 hours.

Makes 4 to 6 servings

MOM'S TUNA CASSEROLE

2 cans (12 ounces *each*) solid albacore tuna, drained and flaked

3 cups diced celery

3 cups crushed potato chips, divided

6 hard-cooked eggs, chopped

1 can (10½ ounces) condensed cream of mushroom soup, undiluted

1 can (10½ ounces) condensed cream of celery soup, undiluted

1 cup mayonnaise

1 teaspoon dried tarragon

1 teaspoon black pepper

1. Combine tuna, celery, 2½ cups potato chips, eggs, soups, mayonnaise, tarragon and pepper in **CROCK-POT®** slow cooker; stir to blend. Cover; cook on LOW 5 to 7 hours.

2. Sprinkle with remaining ½ cup potato chips before serving.

Makes 8 servings

TIP Don't use your **CROCK-POT®** slow cooker to reheat leftover foods. Remove cooled leftover food to a resealable food storage bag or storage container with a tight-fitting lid and refrigerate. Use a microwave oven, the stove top or the oven for reheating.

SWEET POTATO AND PECAN CASSEROLE

1 can (40 ounces) sweet potatoes, drained and mashed

½ cup apple juice

4 tablespoons unsalted butter, melted and divided

½ teaspoon salt

½ teaspoon ground cinnamon

¼ teaspoon black pepper

2 eggs, beaten

⅓ cup packed brown sugar

¼ cup chopped pecans

2 tablespoons all-purpose flour

1. Combine potatoes, apple juice, 2 tablespoons butter, salt, cinnamon and pepper in large bowl. Beat in eggs. Place mixture in **CROCK-POT®** slow cooker.

2. Combine brown sugar, pecans, flour and remaining 2 tablespoons butter in small bowl. Spread over potatoes in **CROCK-POT®** slow cooker. Cover; cook on HIGH 3 to 4 hours.

Makes 8 servings

GREEN BEAN CASSEROLE

2 packages (10 ounces *each*) frozen green beans, thawed

1 can (10¾ ounces) condensed cream of mushroom soup, undiluted

1 tablespoon chopped fresh Italian parsley

1 tablespoon chopped roasted red peppers

1 teaspoon dried sage

½ teaspoon salt

½ teaspoon black pepper

¼ teaspoon ground nutmeg

½ cup toasted slivered almonds*

*To toast almonds, spread in single layer in small skillet. Cook and stir over medium heat 1 to 2 minutes or until nuts are lightly browned.

Combine beans, soup, parsley, red peppers, sage, salt, black pepper and nutmeg in **CROCK-POT**® slow cooker; stir to blend. Cover; cook on LOW 3 to 4 hours. Sprinkle each serving evenly with almonds.

Makes 6 servings

CERVEZA CHICKEN ENCHILADA CASSEROLE

2 cups water

1 stalk celery, chopped

1 small carrot, chopped

1 can (12 ounces) Mexican beer, divided

Juice of 1 lime

1 teaspoon salt

1½ pounds boneless, skinless chicken breasts

1 can (19 ounces) enchilada sauce

7 ounces white corn tortilla chips

½ medium onion, chopped

3 cups (12 ounces) shredded Cheddar cheese

Optional toppings: sour cream, sliced black olives and chopped fresh cilantro

1. Bring water, celery, carrot, 1 cup beer, lime juice and salt to a boil in large saucepan over high heat. Add chicken breasts; reduce heat to simmer. Cook 12 to 14 minutes or until chicken is cooked through. Remove chicken to large cutting board; shred into 1-inch pieces when cool enough to handle.

2. Spread ½ cup enchilada sauce in bottom of **CROCK-POT**® slow cooker. Arrange one third of tortilla chips over sauce. Layer with one third of shredded chicken and one third of chopped onion. Sprinkle with 1 cup cheese. Repeat layers two more times.

3. Pour remaining beer over casserole. Cover; cook on LOW 3½ to 4 hours. Top as desired.

Makes 4 to 6 servings

CHEESY BROCCOLI CASSEROLE

2 packages (10 ounces *each*) frozen chopped broccoli, thawed

1 can (10½ ounces) condensed cream of celery soup, undiluted

1¼ cups (5 ounces) shredded sharp Cheddar cheese, divided

¼ cup minced onion

1 teaspoon paprika

1 teaspoon hot pepper sauce

½ teaspoon celery seeds

1 cup crushed potato chips

1. Coat inside of **CROCK-POT®** slow cooker with nonstick cooking spray. Combine broccoli, soup, 1 cup cheese, onion, paprika, hot pepper sauce and celery seeds in **CROCK-POT®** slow cooker; stir to blend. Cover; cook on LOW 5 to 6 hours or on HIGH 2½ to 3 hours.

2. Uncover; sprinkle top with potato chips and remaining ¼ cup cheese. Cook, uncovered, on LOW 30 to 60 minutes or on HIGH 15 to 30 minutes or until cheese is melted.

Makes 4 to 6 servings

VARIATIONS: Substitute thawed chopped spinach for the broccoli and top with crushed crackers or spicy croutons.

THREE-BEAN CASSEROLE

2 tablespoons olive oil

1 cup chopped onion

1 cup chopped celery

2 cloves garlic, minced

1 can (about 15 ounces) chickpeas, rinsed and drained

1 can (about 15 ounces) kidney beans, rinsed and drained

1 package (10 ounces) frozen cut green beans

1 cup water

1 cup chopped tomato

1 can (8 ounces) tomato sauce

1 to 2 jalapeño peppers, seeded and minced*

1 tablespoon chili powder

2 teaspoons sugar

1½ teaspoons ground cumin

1 teaspoon salt

1 teaspoon dried oregano

¼ teaspoon black pepper

Fresh oregano (optional)

*Jalapeño peppers can sting and irritate the skin, so wear rubber gloves when handling peppers and do not touch your eyes.

1. Heat oil in large skillet over medium heat. Add onion, celery and garlic; cook and stir 5 minutes or until tender. Place in **CROCK-POT**® slow cooker.

2. Add chickpeas, kidney beans, green beans, water, tomato, tomato sauce, jalapeño pepper, chili powder, sugar, cumin, salt, dried oregano and black pepper to **CROCK-POT**® slow cooker; stir to blend. Cover; cook on LOW 6 to 8 hours. Garnish with fresh oregano.

Makes 12 servings

LAYERED MEXICAN-STYLE CASSEROLE

2 cans (about 15 ounces *each*) hominy, drained

1 can (about 15 ounces) black beans, rinsed and drained

1 can (about 14 ounces) diced tomatoes with garlic, basil and oregano

1 cup thick and chunky salsa

1 can (6 ounces) tomato paste

½ teaspoon ground cumin

3 (9-inch) flour tortillas

2 cups (8 ounces) shredded Monterey Jack cheese

¼ cup sliced black olives

1. Prepare foil handles (see Note). Coat inside of **CROCK-POT®** slow cooker with nonstick cooking spray. Combine hominy, beans, tomatoes, salsa, tomato paste and cumin in large bowl; stir to blend.

2. Press 1 tortilla in bottom of **CROCK-POT®** slow cooker. Top with one third of hominy mixture and one third of cheese. Repeat layers. Press remaining tortilla on top. Top with remaining hominy mixture. Set aside remaining one third of cheese.

3. Cover; cook on LOW 6 to 8 hours or on HIGH 2 to 3 hours. Turn off heat. Sprinkle with remaining cheese and olives. Cover; let stand 5 minutes. Pull out tortilla stack with foil handles. Cut into six wedges.

Makes 6 servings

NOTE: To make foil handles, tear off three 18×2-inch strips of heavy-duty foil or use regular foil folded to double thickness. Crisscross foil strips in spoke design and place in **CROCK-POT®** slow cooker to make lifting of tortilla stack easier.

DOWN-HOME SQUASH CASSEROLE

4 cups corn bread stuffing mix (half of 16-ounce package)

½ cup (1 stick) butter, melted

1 can (10¾ ounces) condensed cream of chicken soup, undiluted

¾ cup mayonnaise

¼ cup milk

¼ teaspoon poultry seasoning or rubbed sage

3 medium yellow squash, cut into ½-inch slices (about 1 pound total)

1½ cups frozen seasoning blend vegetables, thawed*

*Seasoning blend is a mixture of chopped bell peppers, onions and celery. If seasoning blend is unavailable, use ½ cup *each* of fresh vegetables.

1. Coat inside of **CROCK-POT**® slow cooker with nonstick cooking spray. Combine stuffing and butter in large bowl; toss gently to coat stuffing thoroughly. Place two-thirds of stuffing in **CROCK-POT**® slow cooker. Place remaining stuffing on plate; set aside.

2. Combine soup, mayonnaise, milk and poultry seasoning in same large bowl. Add squash and vegetables; stir until coated thoroughly. Pour mixture over stuffing mix in **CROCK-POT**® slow cooker. Sprinkle evenly with remaining stuffing.

3. Cover; cook on LOW 4 hours or until squash is tender. Turn off heat. Uncover; let stand 15 minutes before serving.

Makes 8 to 10 servings

TIP Defrost vegetables before cooking them in the **CROCK-POT**® slow cooker.

SLOW COOKER PIZZA CASSEROLE

1½ pounds ground beef

1 pound bulk pork sausage

4 jars (14 ounces *each*) pizza sauce

2 cups (8 ounces) shredded mozzarella cheese

2 cups grated Parmesan cheese

2 cans (4 ounces *each*) mushroom stems and pieces, drained

2 packages (3 ounces *each*) sliced pepperoni

½ cup finely chopped onion

½ cup finely chopped green bell pepper

1 clove garlic, minced

1 pound corkscrew pasta, cooked and drained

1. Brown beef and sausage in large nonstick skillet over medium-high heat 6 to 8 minutes, stirring to break up meat. Drain fat. Remove beef mixture to **CROCK-POT®** slow cooker.

2. Add pizza sauce, cheeses, mushrooms, pepperoni, onion, bell pepper and garlic; stir to blend. Cover; cook on LOW 3½ hours or on HIGH 2 hours.

3. Stir in pasta. Cover; cook on HIGH 15 to 20 minutes or until pasta is heated through.

Makes 6 servings

POLENTA-STYLE CORN CASSEROLE

1 can (about 14 ounces) vegetable broth

½ cup cornmeal

1 can (7 ounces) corn, drained

1 can (4 ounces) diced mild green chiles, drained

¼ cup diced red bell pepper

½ teaspoon salt

¼ teaspoon black pepper

1 cup (4 ounces) shredded Cheddar cheese

1. Pour broth into **CROCK-POT®** slow cooker. Whisk in cornmeal. Add corn, chiles, bell pepper, salt and black pepper. Cover; cook on LOW 4 to 5 hours or on HIGH 2 to 3 hours.

2. Stir in cheese. Cook, uncovered, on LOW 15 to 30 minutes or until cheese is melted.

Makes 6 servings

TIP For firmer polenta, divide cooked corn mixture among lightly greased individual ramekins or spread in pie plate. Cover and refrigerate until firm. Serve cold or at room temperature.

TWISTED CLASSICS

BARBECUE RIBS

Olive oil

2 small red onions, finely chopped

3 to 4 cloves garlic, minced

1 cup packed brown sugar

1 cup ketchup

½ cup cider vinegar

Juice of 1 lemon

2 tablespoons Worcestershire sauce

1 tablespoon hot pepper sauce

½ teaspoon chili powder

2 racks pork baby back ribs, cut into 3- to 4-rib sections

1. Heat oil in large skillet over medium heat. Add onions and garlic; cook and stir 3 to 5 minutes or until softened. Stir in brown sugar, ketchup, vinegar, lemon juice, Worcestershire sauce, hot pepper sauce and chili powder; cook and stir 5 minutes. Remove half of sauce to **CROCK-POT**® slow cooker. Reserve remaining sauce in skillet.

2. Add ribs to **CROCK-POT**® slow cooker; turn to coat. Cover; cook on LOW 7 to 9 hours or on HIGH 4 to 6 hours. Serve ribs with reserved sauce.

Makes 6 servings

PEPPERONI PIZZA MONKEY BREAD

1 package (about 3 ounces) pepperoni, divided

1 teaspoon minced garlic

¼ teaspoon red pepper flakes

1 package (about 16 ounces) refrigerated biscuits, each biscuit cut into 6 pieces

1 can (15 ounces) pizza sauce

1 small green bell pepper, chopped

1 small yellow bell pepper, chopped

1 package (8 ounces) shredded mozzarella cheese

1. Coat inside of **CROCK-POT**® slow cooker with nonstick cooking spray. Prepare foil handles by tearing off four 18×2-inch strips heavy foil (or use regular foil folded to double thickness). Crisscross foil strips in spoke design; place in round **CROCK-POT**® slow cooker. Spray foil handles with nonstick cooking spray.

2. Chop half of pepperoni slices. Combine chopped pepperoni, garlic and red pepper flakes in medium bowl. Roll each biscuit piece into pepperoni mixture; place in **CROCK-POT**® slow cooker. Pour half of pizza sauce over dough. Reserve remaining pizza sauce. Top sauce with bell peppers, mozzarella cheese and remaining half of pepperoni slices.

3. Cover; cook on LOW 3 hours. Turn off heat. Let pizza stand 10 to 15 minutes. Remove from **CROCK-POT**® slow cooker using foil handles. Serve with remaining pizza sauce, if desired.

Makes 12 servings

TURKEY WITH PECAN-CHERRY STUFFING

1 fresh or thawed frozen boneless turkey breast (about 3 to 4 pounds), skin removed

2 cups cooked rice

⅓ cup chopped pecans

⅓ cup dried cherries or cranberries

1 teaspoon poultry seasoning

¼ cup peach, apricot or plum preserves

1 teaspoon Worcestershire sauce

1. Cut slices three-fourths of the way through turkey at 1-inch intervals.

2. Combine rice, pecans, cherries and poultry seasoning in large bowl; stir to blend. Stuff rice mixture between slices. If necessary, skewer turkey lengthwise to hold it together.

3. Place turkey in **CROCK-POT**® slow cooker. Cover; cook on LOW 5 to 6 hours or until turkey registers 170°F on meat thermometer inserted into thickest part of breast, not touching stuffing.

4. Stir together preserves and Worcestershire sauce in small bowl. Spoon over turkey. Turn off heat. Cover; let stand 5 minutes. Remove skewer before serving.

Makes 8 servings

JUICY REUBEN SANDWICHES

1 corned beef, trimmed (about 1½ pounds)

2 cups sauerkraut, drained

½ cup beef broth

1 small onion, sliced

1 clove garlic, minced

¼ teaspoon caraway seeds

4 to 6 black peppercorns

8 slices pumpernickel or rye bread

4 slices Swiss cheese

Prepared mustard

1. Place corned beef, sauerkraut, broth, onion, garlic, caraway seeds and peppercorns in **CROCK-POT®** slow cooker. Cover; cook on LOW 7 to 9 hours.

2. Remove beef to large cutting board. Cut beef across grain into slices. Divide among 4 bread slices. Top each slice with drained sauerkraut mixture and 1 slice cheese. Spread mustard on remaining 4 bread slices; place on sandwiches.

Makes 4 servings

CHICKEN TERIYAKI

1 pound boneless, skinless chicken tenders

1 can (6 ounces) pineapple juice

¼ cup soy sauce

1 tablespoon sugar

1 tablespoon minced fresh ginger

1 tablespoon minced garlic

1 tablespoon vegetable oil

1 tablespoon molasses

24 cherry tomatoes (optional)

2 cups hot cooked rice

Combine chicken, pineapple juice, soy sauce, sugar, ginger, garlic, oil, molasses and tomatoes, if desired, in **CROCK-POT**® slow cooker; stir to blend. Cover; cook on LOW 2 hours or until chicken is tender. Serve chicken and sauce over rice.

Makes 4 servings

STEAMED PORK BUNS

½ (18-ounce) container refrigerated cooked shredded pork in barbecue sauce*

1 tablespoon Asian garlic chili sauce

1 package (about 16 ounces) refrigerated big biscuit dough (8 biscuits)

Dipping Sauce (recipe follows)

Sliced green onions (optional)

*Look for pork in plain, not smoky, barbecue sauce. Substitute chicken in barbecue sauce, if desired.

1. Combine pork and chili sauce in medium bowl. Split biscuits in half. Roll or stretch each biscuit into 4-inch circle. Spoon 1 tablespoon pork onto center of each biscuit. Gather edges around filling and press to seal.

2. Generously butter 2-quart baking dish that fits inside of 5- to 6-quart **CROCK-POT**® slow cooker. Arrange filled biscuits in single layer, overlapping slightly if necessary. Cover dish with buttered foil, butter side down.

3. Place small rack in **CROCK-POT**® slow cooker. Add 1 inch of hot water (water should not touch top of rack). Place baking dish on rack. Cover; cook on HIGH 2 hours.

4. Meanwhile, prepare Dipping Sauce. Garnish pork buns with green onions and serve with Dipping Sauce.

Makes 16 servings

DIPPING SAUCE: Stir together 2 tablespoons rice vinegar, 2 tablespoons soy sauce, 4 teaspoons sugar and 1 teaspoon toasted sesame oil in a small bowl until sugar dissolves. Sprinkle with 1 tablespoon minced green onion just before serving.

TIP **Straight-sided round casserole or soufflé dishes that fit inside the CROCK-POT® stoneware make excellent baking dishes.**

BARBECUED PULLED PORK
SANDWICHES

1 pork shoulder roast (2½ pounds)

1 bottle (14 ounces) barbecue sauce

1 tablespoon lemon juice

1 teaspoon packed brown sugar

1 medium onion, chopped

8 hamburger buns

1. Place pork in **CROCK-POT**® slow cooker. Cover; cook on LOW 10 to 12 hours or on HIGH 5 to 6 hours.

2. Remove pork to large cutting board; shred with two forks. Discard cooking liquid. Return pork to **CROCK-POT**® slow cooker. Add barbecue sauce, lemon juice, brown sugar and onion. Cover; cook on LOW 2 hours or on HIGH 1 hour. Serve on rolls.

Makes 8 servings

TIP For a 5-, 6- or 7-quart **CROCK-POT**® slow cooker, double all ingredients except for the barbecue sauce. Increase the barbecue sauce to 1½ bottles (about 21 ounces total).

MIXED HERB AND
BUTTER RUBBED CHICKEN

3	tablespoons butter, softened	¾	teaspoon salt
1	tablespoon grated lemon peel	¼	teaspoon black pepper
2	teaspoons chopped fresh rosemary	1	whole chicken (4½ to 5 pounds)
1	teaspoon chopped fresh thyme		

1. Coat inside of **CROCK-POT**® slow cooker with nonstick cooking spray. Combine butter, lemon peel, rosemary, thyme, salt and pepper in small bowl; stir to blend. Loosen skin over breast meat and drumsticks; pat chicken dry with paper towels. Rub butter mixture over and under the chicken skin. Place chicken in **CROCK-POT**® slow cooker.

2. Cover; cook on LOW 5 to 6 hours, basting every 30 minutes with cooking liquid. Remove chicken to large cutting board. Let stand 15 minutes before carving.

Makes 4 to 6 servings

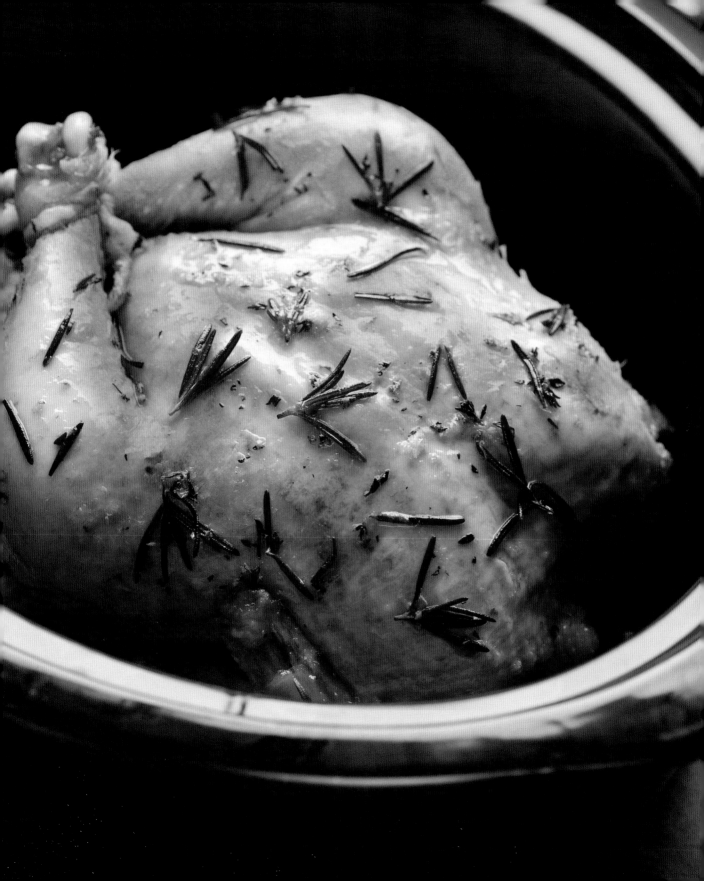

VEGETABLE-STUFFED PORK CHOPS

4 bone-in pork chops
  Salt and black pepper
1 cup frozen corn
1 medium green bell pepper, chopped
½ cup Italian-style seasoned dry bread crumbs

1 small onion, chopped
½ cup uncooked converted long grain rice
1 can (8 ounces) tomato sauce

1. Cut pocket into each pork chop, cutting from edge to bone. Lightly season pockets with salt and black pepper. Combine corn, bell pepper, bread crumbs, onion and rice in large bowl; stir to blend. Stuff pork chops with rice mixture. Secure open side with toothpicks.

2. Place any remaining rice mixture in **CROCK-POT**® slow cooker. Add stuffed pork chops to **CROCK-POT**® slow cooker. Pour tomato sauce over pork chops. Cover; cook on LOW 8 to 10 hours.

3. Remove pork chops to large serving platter. Remove and discard toothpicks. Serve with rice mixture.

Makes 4 servings

TIP Your butcher can cut a pocket in the pork chops to save you time and to ensure even cooking.

BEEFY TOSTADA PIE

2 teaspoons olive oil

1½ cups chopped onion

2 pounds ground beef

1 teaspoon salt

1 teaspoon ground cumin

1 teaspoon chili powder

2 cloves garlic, minced

1 can (15 ounces) tomato sauce

1 cup sliced black olives

8 (6-inch) flour tortillas

3½ cups (14 ounces) shredded Cheddar cheese

Sour cream and chopped green onion (optional)

1. Heat oil in large skillet over medium heat. Add onion; cook and stir 3 to 5 minutes or until tender. Add beef, salt, cumin, chili powder and garlic; cook and stir 6 to 8 minutes or until beef is browned. Drain fat. Stir in tomato sauce; cook until heated through. Stir in olives.

2. Make foil handles using three 18×2-inch strips of heavy-duty foil or use regular foil folded to double thickness. Crisscross foil in spoke design; place across bottom and up side of **CROCK-POT®** slow cooker. Lay 1 tortilla on foil strips. Spread with meat sauce and ½ cup cheese. Top with another tortilla, meat sauce and cheese. Repeat layers five times, ending with tortilla. Cover; cook on HIGH 1½ hours.

3. To serve, lift out of **CROCK-POT®** slow cooker using foil handles and remove to large serving platter. Discard foil. Cut into wedges. Serve with sour cream and green onion, if desired.

Makes 4 to 6 servings

TWISTED CLASSICS

MISO-POACHED SALMON

1½ cups water

2 green onions, cut into 2-inch long pieces, plus additional for garnish

¼ cup yellow miso paste

¼ cup soy sauce

2 tablespoons sake

2 tablespoons mirin

1½ teaspoons grated fresh ginger

1 teaspoon minced garlic

6 (4 ounces *each*) salmon fillets

Hot cooked rice

1. Combine water, 2 green onions, miso paste, soy sauce, sake, mirin, ginger and garlic in **CROCK-POT**® slow cooker; stir to blend. Cover; cook on HIGH 30 minutes.

2. Turn **CROCK-POT**® slow cooker to LOW. Add salmon, skin side down. Cover; cook on LOW 30 to 60 minutes or until salmon turns opaque and flakes easily with fork. Serve over rice with cooking liquid as desired. Garnish with additional green onions.

Makes 6 servings

SLOW COOKER MEAT LOAF

1½ **pounds ground beef**	1 **teaspoon salt**
¾ **cup milk**	½ **teaspoon ground sage**
⅔ **cup fine plain dry bread crumbs**	½ **cup ketchup**
2 **eggs, beaten**	2 **tablespoons packed brown sugar**
2 **tablespoons minced onion**	1 **teaspoon dry mustard**

1. Combine beef, milk, bread crumbs, eggs, onion, salt and sage in large bowl; shape into loaf. Place meat loaf in **CROCK-POT**® slow cooker. Cover; cook on LOW 5 to 6 hours.

2. Turn **CROCK-POT**® slow cooker to HIGH. Combine ketchup, brown sugar and dry mustard in small bowl; pour over meat loaf in **CROCK-POT**® slow cooker. Cover; cook on HIGH 15 minutes.

Makes 6 servings

TWISTED CLASSICS

SHREDDED CHICKEN TACOS

2 pounds boneless, skinless chicken thighs	8 (6-inch) yellow corn tortillas, warmed
½ cup prepared mango salsa, plus additional for serving	Lettuce (optional)

1. Coat inside of **CROCK-POT**® slow cooker with nonstick cooking spray. Add chicken and ½ cup salsa. Cover; cook on LOW 4 to 5 hours or on HIGH 2½ to 3 hours.

2. Remove chicken to large cutting board; shred with two forks. Stir shredded chicken into **CROCK-POT**® slow cooker. To serve, divide chicken, lettuce, if desired, and additional salsa evenly among tortillas.

Makes 4 servings

STUFFED CHICKEN BREASTS

6 boneless, skinless chicken breasts

8 ounces feta cheese, crumbled

3 cups chopped fresh spinach leaves

⅓ cup sun-dried tomatoes packed in oil, drained and chopped

1 teaspoon minced lemon peel

1 teaspoon dried basil, oregano or mint

½ teaspoon garlic powder

Black pepper

1 can (about 14 ounces) diced tomatoes

½ cup oil-cured olives*

Hot cooked polenta

Lemon peel twists (optional)

*If using pitted olives, add to **CROCK-POT**® slow cooker during last hour of cooking.

1. Place 1 chicken breast between two pieces of plastic wrap. Using tenderizer mallet or back of skillet, pound until about ¼ inch thick. Repeat with remaining chicken.

2. Combine feta, spinach, sun-dried tomatoes, lemon peel, basil, garlic powder and pepper in medium bowl.

3. Place chicken breasts, smooth sides down, on work surface. Place 2 tablespoons feta mixture on wide end of each breast. Roll tightly.

4. Place rolled chicken, seam sides down, in **CROCK-POT**® slow cooker. Top with tomatoes and olives. Cover; cook on LOW 5½ to 6 hours or on HIGH 4 hours. Serve over polenta. Garnish with lemon peel.

Makes 6 servings

HOLIDAY HAM

1 bone-in cooked ham (about 5 to 7 pounds), trimmed*

16 whole cloves

1 cup water

1½ teaspoons vegetable oil

1 shallot, chopped

1 jar (12 ounces) cherry preserves or currant jelly

¾ cup dried orange-flavored cranberries or raisins

½ cup packed brown sugar

½ cup orange juice

½ teaspoon dry mustard

*Unless you have a 5-, 6- or 7-quart **CROCK-POT®** slow cooker, cut any piece of meat larger than 2½ pounds in half so it cooks completely.

1. Score ham. Place 1 clove in center of each diamond. Pour water into **CROCK-POT®** slow cooker; add ham. Cover; cook on LOW 5 to 6 hours or on HIGH 2½ to 3 hours.

2. Heat oil in small saucepan over medium-high heat. Add shallot; cook and stir 2 to 3 minutes or until translucent. Stir in preserves, cranberries, brown sugar, orange juice and dry mustard. Reduce heat to medium; cook until sugar is dissolved.

3. Remove ham from **CROCK-POT®** slow cooker; drain liquid. Place ham back into **CROCK-POT®** slow cooker; pour preserve mixture over ham. Cover; cook on HIGH 10 to 20 minutes or until fruit plumps.

Makes 12 to 14 servings

CHICKEN CACCIATORE

4 teaspoons olive oil

3 pounds boneless, skinless chicken breasts

½ teaspoon salt

¼ teaspoon black pepper

½ medium red bell pepper, sliced

½ medium green bell pepper, sliced

½ medium yellow bell pepper, sliced

1 cup onion, sliced

14 grape tomatoes

1½ cups water

¼ cup all-purpose flour

2 teaspoons garlic powder

1 teaspoon ground cumin

1 teaspoon dried oregano

1 teaspoon paprika

⅛ teaspoon ground red pepper

Hot cooked noodles or rice (optional)

1. Heat 2 teaspoons oil in large skillet over medium-high heat. Sprinkle chicken with salt and black pepper. Add half of chicken to skillet; cook 4 minutes per side or until browned. Remove to large plate. Repeat with remaining 2 teaspoons oil and chicken.

2. Add bell peppers, onion and grape tomatoes to 5- to 6-quart **CROCK-POT**® slow cooker. Combine water, flour, garlic powder, cumin, oregano, paprika and ground red pepper in medium bowl; mix well. Add to **CROCK-POT**® slow cooker. Top with chicken. Cover; cook on LOW 8 to 9 hours or on HIGH 4 to 4½ hours. Serve over noodles, if desired.

Makes 6 servings

CORNISH HENS FOR TWO

1 head garlic, divided

1 lemon, cut in half

2 Cornish game hens (1 pound *each*)

   Salt and black pepper

2 large portobella mushrooms

2 medium onions, thinly sliced

1 can (10½ ounces) cream of chicken soup

2 tablespoons fresh Italian parsley, thyme and/or sage

   Hot mashed potatoes, rice or egg noodles (optional)

1. Coat inside of **CROCK-POT**® slow cooker with nonstick cooking spray. Cut head of garlic in half; separate cloves. Reserve half of whole cloves; mince remaining half of cloves. Place ¼ whole cloves garlic and lemon half into each chicken; season with salt and pepper.

2. Place mushrooms, stem side up, onions and minced garlic in **CROCK-POT**® slow cooker; top with chicken, soup and herbs. Cover; cook on LOW 6 hours or on HIGH 3 hours, turning chicken halfway through cooking time. Serve over mashed potatoes, if desired.

Makes 2 servings

ON THE SIDE

PARMESAN RANCH SNACK MIX

3 cups corn or rice cereal squares

2 cups oyster crackers

1 package (5 ounces) bagel chips, broken in half

1½ cups mini pretzel twists

1 cup pistachio nuts

2 tablespoons grated Parmesan cheese

¼ cup (½ stick) butter, melted

1 package (1 ounce) dry ranch salad dressing mix

½ teaspoon garlic powder

1. Combine cereal, crackers, bagel chips, pretzels, nuts and cheese in **CROCK-POT**® slow cooker; mix gently.

2. Combine butter, salad dressing mix and garlic powder in small bowl. Pour over cereal mixture; toss lightly to coat. Cover; cook on LOW 3 hours.

3. Stir gently. Cook, uncovered, on LOW 30 minutes.

Makes about 9½ cups

CHICKEN AND ASIAGO STUFFED MUSHROOMS

20 large white mushrooms, stems removed and reserved

3 tablespoons extra virgin olive oil, divided

¼ cup finely chopped onion

2 cloves garlic, minced

¼ cup Madeira wine

½ pound chicken sausage, casings removed or ground chicken

1 cup grated Asiago cheese

¼ cup Italian-style seasoned dry bread crumbs

3 tablespoons chopped fresh Italian parsley

½ teaspoon salt

¼ teaspoon black pepper

1. Lightly brush mushroom caps with 1 tablespoon oil; set aside. Finely chop mushroom stems.

2. Heat remaining 2 tablespoons oil in large nonstick skillet over medium-high heat. Add onion; cook about 1 minute or until just beginning to soften. Add mushroom stems; cook 5 to 6 minutes or until beginning to brown. Stir in garlic; cook 1 minute.

3. Pour in wine; cook 1 minute. Add sausage; cook 3 to 4 minutes or until no longer pink, stirring to break into small pieces. Remove from heat; cool 5 minutes. Stir in cheese, bread crumbs, parsley, salt and pepper.

4. Divide mushroom-sausage mixture among mushroom caps, pressing slightly to compress. Place stuffed mushroom caps in single layer in **CROCK-POT**® slow cooker. Cover; cook on LOW 4 hours or on HIGH 2 hours or until mushrooms are tender and filling is cooked through.

Makes 4 to 5 servings

TIP Stuffed mushrooms are a great way to impress guests with your gourmet cooking skills. These appetizers appear time intensive and fancy, but they are actually simple with the help of a **CROCK-POT**® slow cooker.

CORN ON THE COB WITH GARLIC HERB BUTTER

4 to 5 ears of corn, husked

½ cup (1 stick) unsalted butter, softened

3 to 4 cloves garlic, minced

2 tablespoons finely minced fresh Italian parsley

Salt and black pepper

1. Place each ear of corn on piece of foil. Combine butter, garlic and parsley in small bowl; spread onto corn. Season with salt and pepper; tightly seal foil.

2. Place in **CROCK-POT®** slow cooker, overlapping ears, if necessary. Add enough water to come one fourth of the way up each ear. Cover; cook on LOW 4 to 5 hours or on HIGH 2 to 2½ hours.

Makes 4 to 5 servings

CARAMELIZED ONION DIP

1 tablespoon olive oil

1½ cups chopped sweet onion

1 teaspoon sugar

⅛ teaspoon dried thyme

¼ teaspoon salt

2 ounces cream cheese, cubed

½ cup sour cream

⅓ cup mayonnaise

⅓ cup (about 1 ounce) shredded Swiss cheese

¼ teaspoon beef soup base or beef bouillon granules

Potato chips and carrot sticks

1. Heat oil in medium skillet over medium heat. Add onion, sugar and thyme; cook 12 minutes or until golden, stirring occasionally. Stir in salt.

2. Coat inside of **CROCK-POT® LITTLE DIPPER®** slow cooker with nonstick cooking spray. Add onion mixture, cream cheese, sour cream, mayonnaise, Swiss cheese and beef base; mix well. Cover; heat 1 hour or until warm. Stir to blend. Serve with potato chips and carrot sticks.

Makes 12 servings

STEAMED ARTICHOKES
WITH THREE SAUCES

4 artichokes, trimmed and cut in
   half

Juice of ½ lemon

Dipping Sauces (recipes follow)

Place trimmed artichokes cut side down in bottom of **CROCK-POT**® slow cooker. Add enough water to come halfway up artichokes; add lemon juice. Cover; cook on LOW 6 hours. Serve with one or more Dipping Sauces.

Makes 8 servings

TARRAGON BROWNED
BUTTER DIPPING SAUCE

1 cup (2 sticks) butter

4 teaspoons dried tarragon *or*
   ¼ cup finely chopped fresh
   tarragon

Melt butter in medium saucepan over medium heat. Cook, swirling butter in saucepan over heat until butter is light brown. Remove from heat and stir in tarragon. Cover to keep warm.

CREAM CHEESE-BACON DIPPING SAUCE

4 ounces cream cheese

1 cup whipping cream

½ teaspoon black pepper

8 slices bacon, crisp-cooked and
   finely chopped

Whisk cream cheese and cream in medium saucepan over medium heat until smooth. Stir in pepper and bacon. Cover to keep warm.

GARLIC-HERB BUTTER DIPPING SAUCE

1 cup (2 sticks) butter

8 cloves garlic, crushed

½ cup chopped fresh herbs such as Italian parsley, tarragon or chives

Melt butter in medium saucepan over medium heat. Add garlic and cook, stirring frequently, until garlic is golden brown. Remove from heat. Strain garlic from sauce and stir in herbs. Cover to keep warm.

ON THE SIDE

CURRIED SNACK MIX

3 tablespoons butter

2 tablespoons packed light brown sugar

1½ teaspoons hot curry powder

¼ teaspoon ground cumin

¼ teaspoon salt

2 cups rice cereal squares

1 cup walnut halves

1 cup dried cranberries

Melt butter in large skillet. Add brown sugar, curry powder, cumin and salt; mix well. Add cereal, walnuts and cranberries; stir to coat. Remove mixture to **CROCK-POT**® slow cooker. Cover; cook on LOW 3 hours. Uncover; cook on LOW 30 minutes.

Makes 16 servings

MUSHROOM WILD RICE

1½ cups vegetable broth

1 cup uncooked wild rice

½ cup diced onion

½ cup sliced mushrooms

½ cup diced red or green bell pepper

1 tablespoon olive oil

Salt and black pepper

Combine broth, rice, onion, mushrooms, bell pepper, oil, salt and black pepper in **CROCK-POT**® slow cooker; stir to blend. Cover; cook on HIGH 2½ hours or until rice is tender and liquid is absorbed.

Makes 8 servings

CINNAMON ROLL AND SWEET 'TATER GRATIN

3 pounds sweet potatoes, cut into ¼-inch thick rounds

¾ cup (3 ounces) shredded mozzarella cheese

1 cup whipping cream

¼ to ½ teaspoon ground red pepper

Salt and black pepper

4 tablespoons (½ stick) butter, cubed and divided

1 can (about 12 ounces) refrigerated cinnamon roll dough

1. Coat inside of **CROCK-POT®** slow cooker with nonstick cooking spray. Arrange one third of potatoes in **CROCK-POT®** slow cooker, overlapping slightly. Top with ¼ cup cheese. Repeat layers two additional times using potatoes and cheese.

2. Combine cream, ground red pepper, salt and black pepper in small bowl; stir to blend. Pour cream mixture over potato layers in **CROCK-POT®** slow cooker. Dot with 2 tablespoons butter.

3. Remove cinnamon roll dough from can; unroll into long strips. Set aside icing. Arrange strips of dough in lattice design on top of potato layers, making sure edges are sealed. Dot dough with remaining 2 tablespoons butter. Cover; cook on HIGH 4 hours.

4. Turn off heat. Drizzle gratin with reserved icing. Let stand, uncovered, 15 minutes before serving.

Makes 10 servings

BACON-WRAPPED FINGERLING POTATOES

1 pound fingerling potatoes

2 tablespoons olive oil

1 tablespoon minced fresh thyme

½ teaspoon black pepper

¼ teaspoon paprika

½ pound bacon slices, cut crosswise into halves

¼ cup chicken broth

1. Toss potatoes with oil, thyme, pepper and paprika in large bowl. Wrap half slice of bacon tightly around each potato.

2. Heat large skillet over medium heat; add potatoes. Reduce heat to medium-low; cook until lightly browned and bacon has tightened around potatoes. Place potatoes in **CROCK-POT®** slow cooker. Add broth. Cover; cook on HIGH 3 hours.

Makes 4 to 6 servings

CHEESY POLENTA

6 cups vegetable broth

1½ cups uncooked medium-grind instant polenta

½ cup grated Parmesan cheese, plus additional for garnish

4 tablespoons (½ stick) unsalted butter, cubed

Fried sage leaves (optional)

1. Coat inside of **CROCK-POT®** slow cooker with nonstick cooking spray. Heat broth in large saucepan over high heat. Remove to **CROCK-POT®** slow cooker; whisk in polenta.

2. Cover; cook on LOW 2 to 2½ hours or until polenta is tender and creamy. Stir in ½ cup cheese and butter. Serve with additional cheese. Garnish with sage.

Makes 6 servings

TIP Spread any leftover polenta in a baking dish and refrigerate until cold. Cut cold polenta into sticks or slices. You can then fry or grill the polenta until lightly browned.

ROSEMARY-OLIVE FOCACCIA

1 cup warm water (100° to 110°F)

3 tablespoons extra virgin olive oil

3 packets (¼ ounce *each*) active dry yeast

1 tablespoon sugar

3 cups all-purpose flour

½ cup pitted kalamata olives, chopped

1 tablespoon plus 1 to 2 teaspoons chopped fresh rosemary, divided

1 teaspoon salt

¼ teaspoon red pepper flakes (optional)

1. Combine water, oil, yeast and sugar in medium bowl; let stand 5 minutes. Combine flour, olives, 1 tablespoon rosemary and salt in large bowl. Pour water mixture into flour mixture; stir until rough dough forms. Turn dough out onto floured surface; knead about 5 to 6 minutes or until smooth. Place dough in oiled bowl, turning to coat surface. Cover with plastic wrap and let stand in a warm place about 1½ hours or until doubled in size.

2. Punch down dough. Coat inside of oval 6-quart **CROCK-POT®** slow cooker with nonstick cooking spray. Add dough; press down and stretch to fit. Sprinkle with remaining 1 to 2 teaspoons rosemary and red pepper flakes, if desired. Cover; cook on HIGH 1½ to 2 hours or until dough is puffed and lightly browned on the sides. Remove to wire rack; let cool 10 minutes before cutting into wedges.

Makes 1 loaf

CAULIFLOWER MASH

2 heads cauliflower (8 cups florets)
1 tablespoon butter
1 tablespoon milk

Salt
Sprigs fresh Italian parsley (optional)

1. Arrange cauliflower in **CROCK-POT**® slow cooker. Add enough water to fill **CROCK-POT**® slow cooker by about 2 inches. Cover; cook on LOW 5 to 6 hours. Drain well.

2. Place cooked cauliflower in food processor or blender; process until almost smooth. Add butter; process until smooth. Add milk as needed to reach desired consistency. Season with salt. Garnish with parsley.

Makes 6 servings

NO-FUSS MACARONI AND CHEESE

2 cups (about 8 ounces) uncooked elbow macaroni

3 ounces pasteurized process cheese product, cubed

1 cup (4 ounces) shredded mild Cheddar cheese

½ teaspoon salt

⅛ teaspoon black pepper

1½ cups milk

Combine macaroni, cheese product, Cheddar cheese, salt and pepper in **CROCK-POT**® slow cooker; pour milk over top. Cover; cook on LOW 2 to 3 hours, stirring halfway through cooking time.

Makes 8 servings

FIVE-INGREDIENT MUSHROOM STUFFING

6 tablespoons unsalted butter

2 medium onions, chopped

1 pound sliced white mushrooms

¼ teaspoon salt

5 cups bagged stuffing mix, any seasoning

1 cup vegetable broth

Chopped fresh Italian parsley (optional)

1. Melt butter in large skillet over medium-high heat. Add onions, mushrooms and salt; cook and stir 20 minutes or until vegetables are browned and most liquid is absorbed. Remove onion mixture to **CROCK-POT®** slow cooker.

2. Stir in stuffing mix and broth. Cover; cook on LOW 3 hours. Garnish with parsley.

Makes 12 servings

CEREAL SNACK MIX

6 tablespoons unsalted butter, melted

2 tablespoons curry powder

2 tablespoons soy sauce

1 tablespoon sugar

1 tablespoon paprika

2 teaspoons ground cumin

½ teaspoon salt

5 cups rice squares cereal

5 cups corn squares cereal

1 cup tiny pretzels

⅓ cup peanuts

1. Pour butter into **CROCK-POT**® slow cooker. Stir in curry powder, soy sauce, sugar, paprika, cumin and salt. Stir in cereal, pretzels and peanuts. Cook, uncovered, on HIGH 45 minutes, stirring often.

2. Turn **CROCK-POT**® slow cooker to LOW. Cook, uncovered, on LOW 3 to 4 hours, stirring often. Turn off heat. Let cool completely.

Makes 20 servings

TIP The Cereal Snack Mix needs to be stirred often while cooking in order to prevent it from scorching.

SPINACH GORGONZOLA CORN BREAD

2 boxes (8½ ounces *each*) corn bread mix

1 box (10 ounces) frozen chopped spinach, thawed and drained

1 cup crumbled Gorgonzola cheese

3 eggs

½ cup whipping cream

1 teaspoon black pepper

Paprika (optional)

1. Coat inside of 5-quart **CROCK-POT**® slow cooker with nonstick cooking spray. Combine corn bread mix, spinach, cheese, eggs, cream, pepper and paprika, if desired, in medium bowl; stir to blend. Place batter in **CROCK-POT**® slow cooker.

2. Cover; cook on HIGH 1½ hours. Turn off heat. Let bread cool completely before inverting onto large serving platter.

Makes 1 loaf

NOTE: Cook only on HIGH setting for proper crust and texture.

RUSTIC CHEDDAR MASHED POTATOES

2 pounds russet potatoes, diced

1 cup water

2 tablespoons unsalted butter, cubed

¾ cup milk

¾ teaspoon salt

½ teaspoon black pepper

½ cup finely chopped green onions

2 tablespoons shredded Cheddar cheese

1. Combine potatoes, water and butter in **CROCK-POT**® slow cooker. Cover; cook on LOW 6 hours or on HIGH 3 hours. Remove potatoes to large bowl using slotted spoon.

2. Beat potatoes with electric mixer at medium speed 2 to 3 minutes or until well blended. Add milk, salt and pepper; beat 2 minutes or until well blended.

3. Stir in green onions and cheese. Turn off heat. Cover; let stand 15 minutes or until cheese is melted.

Makes 8 servings

DAZZLING DESSERTS

TRIPLE WHITE CHOCOLATE FANTASY

2 pounds white almond bark, broken into pieces

1 bar (4 ounces) white chocolate, broken into pieces*

1 package (12 ounces) white chocolate chips

3 cups candy-coated chocolate pieces or colored sprinkles

*Use your favorite high-quality chocolate candy bar.

1. Place almond bark, chocolate bar and chocolate chips in **CROCK-POT**® slow cooker. Cover; cook on HIGH 1 hour. *Do not stir.*

2. Turn **CROCK-POT**® slow cooker to LOW. Cover; cook on LOW 1 hour, stirring every 15 minutes. Stir in chocolate pieces.

3. Spread mixture onto large baking sheet covered with waxed paper; cool completely. Break into pieces. Store in tightly covered container.

Makes 36 pieces

VARIATIONS: Here are a few ideas for other imaginative items to add in along with or instead of the candy-coated chocolate pieces: raisins, crushed peppermint candy, crushed toffee, peanuts or pistachio nuts, chopped gum drops, chopped dried fruit or candied cherries.

BITTERSWEET CHOCOLATE-ESPRESSO CRÈME BRÛLÉE

½ cup chopped bittersweet chocolate

5 egg yolks

1½ cups whipping cream

½ cup granulated sugar

¼ cup espresso

¼ cup Demerara or raw sugar

1. Arrange five 6-ounce ramekins or custard cups inside of **CROCK-POT**® slow cooker. Pour enough water to come halfway up sides of ramekins (taking care to keep water out of ramekins). Divide chocolate among ramekins.

2. Whisk egg yolks in small bowl; set aside. Heat small saucepan over medium heat. Add cream, granulated sugar and espresso; cook and stir until mixture begins to boil. Pour hot cream in thin, steady stream into egg yolks, whisking constantly. Pour through fine mesh strainer into clean bowl.

3. Ladle into prepared ramekins over chocolate. Cover; cook on HIGH 1 to 2 hours or until custard is set around edges but still soft in centers. Carefully remove ramekins; cool to room temperature. Cover and refrigerate until serving.

4. Spread tops of custards with Demerara sugar just before serving. Serve immediately.

Makes 5 servings

ROCKY ROAD BROWNIE BOTTOMS

½ cup packed brown sugar

½ cup water

2 tablespoons unsweetened cocoa powder

2½ cups packaged brownie mix

1 package (about 4 ounces) instant chocolate pudding mix

½ cup milk chocolate chips

2 eggs, beaten

3 tablespoons butter or margarine, melted

2 cups mini marshmallows

1 cup chopped pecans or walnuts, toasted*

½ cup chocolate syrup

*To toast pecans, spread in a single layer on small baking sheet. Bake in preheated 350°F oven 5 to 7 minutes or until fragrant, stirring frequently.

1. Coat inside of **CROCK-POT**® slow cooker with nonstick cooking spray. Prepare foil handles by tearing off four 18×2-inch strips heavy foil (or use regular foil folded to double thickness). Crisscross foil strips in spoke design; place in round **CROCK-POT**® slow cooker. Spray foil handles with nonstick cooking spray. Combine brown sugar, water and cocoa in small saucepan over medium heat; bring to a boil over medium-high heat.

2. Meanwhile, combine brownie mix, pudding mix, chocolate chips, eggs and butter in medium bowl; stir until well blended. Spread batter in **CROCK-POT**® slow cooker; pour boiling sugar mixture over batter.

3. Cover; cook on HIGH 1½ hours. Turn off heat. Top brownies with marshmallows, pecans and chocolate syrup. Let stand 15 minutes.

Makes 6 servings

NOTE: Recipe can be doubled for a 5-, 6- or 7-quart **CROCK-POT**® slow cooker.

CINNAMON ROLL-TOPPED MIXED BERRY COBBLER

- 2 bags (12 ounces *each*) frozen mixed berries, thawed
- 1 cup sugar
- ¼ cup quick-cooking tapioca
- ¼ cup water
- 2 teaspoons vanilla
- 1 package (about 12 ounces) refrigerated cinnamon rolls with icing

Combine berries, sugar, tapioca, water and vanilla in **CROCK-POT**® slow cooker; top with cinnamon rolls. Cover; cook on LOW 4 to 5 hours. Serve warm; drizzled with icing.

Makes 8 servings

NOTE: This recipe was designed to work best in a 4-quart **CROCK-POT**® slow cooker. Double the ingredients for larger **CROCK-POT**® slow cookers, but always place cinnamon rolls in a single layer.

CHERRY DELIGHT

1 can (21 ounces) cherry pie filling

1 package (about 18 ounces) yellow cake mix

½ cup (1 stick) butter, melted

⅓ cup chopped walnuts

Place pie filling in **CROCK-POT**® slow cooker. Combine cake mix and butter in medium bowl. Spread evenly over pie filling. Sprinkle with walnuts. Cover; cook on LOW 3 to 4 hours or on HIGH 1½ to 2 hours.

Makes 8 to 10 servings

CHOCOLATE ORANGE FONDUE

½ cup whipping cream

1½ tablespoons butter

6 ounces 60 to 70% bittersweet chocolate, coarsely chopped

⅓ cup orange liqueur

¾ teaspoon vanilla

Marshmallows, strawberries and pound cake cubes

1. Bring cream and butter to a boil in medium saucepan over medium heat. Remove from heat. Stir in chocolate, liqueur and vanilla until chocolate is melted. Place over medium-low heat; cook and stir 2 minutes until smooth.

2. Coat inside of **CROCK-POT® LITTLE DIPPER®** slow cooker with nonstick cooking spray. Fill with warm fondue. Serve with marshmallows, strawberries and pound cake cubes.

Makes 1½ cups

PEANUT FUDGE PUDDING CAKE

1 cup all-purpose flour	1 teaspoon vanilla
1 cup sugar, divided	¼ cup unsweetened cocoa powder
1½ teaspoons baking powder	1 cup boiling water
⅔ cup milk	Chopped peanuts (optional)
½ cup peanut butter	Vanilla ice cream (optional)
2 tablespoons vegetable oil	

1. Coat inside of 5-quart **CROCK-POT**® slow cooker with nonstick cooking spray. Combine flour, ½ cup sugar and baking powder in medium bowl. Stir in milk, peanut butter, oil and vanilla until well blended. Pour batter into **CROCK-POT**® slow cooker.

2. Combine remaining ½ cup sugar and cocoa in small bowl. Stir in water. Pour into **CROCK-POT**® slow cooker. *Do not stir.*

3. Cover; cook on HIGH 1¼ to 1½ hours or until toothpick inserted into center comes out clean. Turn off heat. Let stand 10 minutes; scoop into serving dishes or invert onto large serving platter. Serve warm with chopped peanuts and ice cream, if desired.

Makes 4 servings

TIP Because this recipe makes its own fudge topping, be sure to spoon some of it from the bottom of the **CROCK-POT**® slow cooker when serving, or invert the cake for a luscious chocolately finish.

HOT FUDGE CAKE

1½ cups packed light brown sugar, divided

2 cups all-purpose flour

¼ cup plus 3 tablespoons unsweetened cocoa powder, divided, plus additional for dusting

2 teaspoons baking powder

1 teaspoon salt

1 cup milk

¼ cup (½ stick) butter, melted

1 teaspoon vanilla

3½ cups boiling water

1. Coat inside of 5-quart **CROCK-POT®** slow cooker with nonstick cooking spray. Prepare foil handles by tearing off four 18×2-inch strips heavy foil (or use regular foil folded to double thickness). Crisscross foil strips in spoke design; place in round **CROCK-POT®** slow cooker. Spray foil handles with nonstick cooking spray. Mix 1 cup brown sugar, flour, 3 tablespoons cocoa, baking powder and salt in medium bowl. Stir in milk, butter and vanilla; mix until well blended. Pour into **CROCK-POT®** slow cooker.

2. Blend remaining ½ cup brown sugar and ¼ cup cocoa in small bowl. Sprinkle evenly over mixture in **CROCK-POT®** slow cooker. Pour in boiling water. *Do not stir.*

3. Cover; cook on HIGH 1¼ to 1½ hours or until toothpick inserted into center comes out clean. Turn off heat. Let stand 10 minutes. Invert onto large serving platter or scoop into individual serving dishes. Dust with additional cocoa.

Makes 6 to 8 servings

SPIKED SPONGE CAKE

1 package (about 18 ounces) yellow cake mix

1 cup water

4 eggs

½ cup vegetable oil

1 tablespoon grated orange peel

1 package (6 ounces) golden raisins and cherries or other chopped dried fruit (about 1 cup)

1 cup chopped pecans

½ cup sugar

½ cup (1 stick) butter

¼ cup bourbon or apple juice

1. Coat inside of 5-quart **CROCK-POT**® slow cooker with nonstick cooking spray.

2. Combine cake mix, water, eggs and oil in large bowl; stir to blend. (Batter will be lumpy). Stir in orange peel. Pour two thirds of batter into **CROCK-POT**® slow cooker. Sprinkle dried fruit evenly over batter. Top evenly with remaining batter. Cover; cook on HIGH 1½ to 1¾ hours or until toothpick inserted into center of cake comes out clean.

3. Immediately remove stoneware and cool 10 minutes on wire rack. Run flat rubber spatula around edge of cake, lifting bottom slightly. Invert onto large serving plate.

4. Heat large skillet over medium-high heat. Add pecans; cook and stir 2 to 3 minutes or until pecans are golden brown. Add sugar, butter and bourbon; bring to a boil, stirring constantly. Cook 1 to 2 minutes or until sugar dissolves. Pour over cake.

Makes 8 to 10 servings

TIP Allow breads, cakes and puddings to cool at least 5 minutes before scooping or removing them from the **CROCK-POT**® slow cooker.

DAZZLING DESSERTS

PUMPKIN CUSTARD

1 cup solid-pack pumpkin	½ teaspoon grated lemon peel
½ cup packed brown sugar	½ teaspoon ground cinnamon, plus additional for garnish
2 eggs, beaten	
½ teaspoon ground ginger	1 can (12 ounces) evaporated milk

1. Combine pumpkin, brown sugar, eggs, ginger, lemon peel and ½ teaspoon cinnamon in large bowl. Stir in evaporated milk. Divide mixture among six ramekins or custard cups. Cover each cup tightly with foil.

2. Place ramekins in **CROCK-POT®** slow cooker. Pour water into **CROCK-POT®** slow cooker to come about ½ inch from top of ramekins. Cover; cook on LOW 4 hours.

3. Use tongs or slotted spoon to remove ramekins from **CROCK-POT®** slow cooker. Sprinkle with additional ground cinnamon. Serve warm.

Makes 6 servings

VARIATION: To make Pumpkin Custard in a single dish, pour custard into 1½-quart soufflé dish instead of ramekins. Cover with foil; place in **CROCK-POT®** slow cooker. (Place soufflé dish on two or three 18×2-inch strips of foil in **CROCK-POT®** slow cooker to make removal easier, if desired.) Add water to come 1½ inches from top of the soufflé dish. Cover; cook as directed above.

TRIPLE CHOCOLATE FANTASY

2 pounds white almond bark, broken into pieces

1 bar (4 ounces) sweetened chocolate, broken into pieces*

1 package (12 ounces) semisweet chocolate chips

2 cups coarsely chopped pecans, toasted**

*Use your favorite high-quality chocolate candy bar.

**To toast pecans, spread in single layer in heavy skillet. Cook and stir over medium heat 1 to 2 minutes or until nuts are lightly browned.

1. Line mini muffin pan with mini muffin cups. Place bark, sweetened chocolate and chocolate chips in **CROCK-POT®** slow cooker. Cover; cook on HIGH 1 hour. *Do not stir.*

2. Turn **CROCK-POT®** slow cooker to LOW. Cover; cook on LOW 1 hour, stirring every 15 minutes. Stir in nuts.

3. Drop mixture by tablespoonfuls into prepared muffin pan cups; cool. Store in tightly covered container.

Makes 36 pieces

VARIATIONS: Here are a few ideas for other imaginative items to add in along with or instead of the pecans: raisins, crushed peppermint candy, candy-coated baking bits, crushed toffee, peanuts or pistachio nuts, chopped gum drops, chopped dried fruit, candied cherries, chopped marshmallows or sweetened coconut.

CHOCOLATE HAZELNUT
PUDDING CAKE

1 box (about 18 ounces) golden yellow cake mix

1 cup water

4 eggs

½ cup sour cream

½ cup vegetable oil

1 cup mini semisweet chocolate chips

½ cup chopped hazelnuts

Whipped cream or ice cream (optional)

1. Coat inside of 6-quart **CROCK-POT**® slow cooker with nonstick cooking spray. Combine cake mix, water, eggs, sour cream and oil; stir until smooth. Pour batter into **CROCK-POT**® slow cooker. Cover; cook on HIGH 2 hours or until batter is nearly set.

2. Sprinkle on mini chocolate chips and hazelnuts. Cover; cook on HIGH 30 minutes or until toothpick inserted into center comes out clean or cake begins to pull away from sides of **CROCK-POT**® slow cooker. Turn off heat. Let stand until cooled slightly. Slice or spoon out while warm. Serve with whipped cream, if desired.

Makes 10 servings

TEQUILA-POACHED PEARS

4 Anjou pears, peeled
2 cups water
1 can (11½ ounces) pear nectar
1 cup tequila
½ cup sugar
Grated peel and juice of 1 lime
Vanilla ice cream (optional)

1. Place pears in **CROCK-POT®** slow cooker. Combine water, nectar, tequila, sugar, lime peel and lime juice in medium saucepan. Bring to a boil over medium-high heat, stirring frequently. Boil 1 minute; pour over pears.

2. Cover; cook on LOW 4 to 6 hours or on HIGH 2 to 3 hours or until pears are tender. Serve warm with poaching liquid and vanilla ice cream, if desired.

Makes 4 servings

TIP Poaching fruit in a sugar, juice or alcohol syrup helps the fruit retain its shape and become more flavorful.

DAZZLING DESSERTS

FUDGE AND CREAM PUDDING CAKE

- 2 tablespoons unsalted butter
- 1 cup all-purpose flour
- ½ cup packed light brown sugar
- 5 tablespoons unsweetened cocoa powder, divided
- 2 teaspoons baking powder
- ½ teaspoon ground cinnamon
- ⅛ teaspoon salt

- 1 cup light cream
- 1 tablespoon vegetable oil
- 1 teaspoon vanilla
- 1½ cups hot water
- ½ cup packed dark brown sugar
- Whipped cream or ice cream (optional)

1. Coat inside of 5-quart **CROCK-POT**® slow cooker with butter. Combine flour, light brown sugar, 3 tablespoons cocoa, baking powder, cinnamon and salt in medium bowl. Add cream, oil and vanilla; stir well to combine. Pour batter into **CROCK-POT**® slow cooker.

2. Combine hot water, dark brown sugar and remaining 2 tablespoons cocoa in medium bowl; stir well. Pour sauce over cake batter. *Do not stir.* Cover; cook on HIGH 2 hours.

3. Spoon pudding cake into bowls. Serve with whipped cream, if desired.

Makes 8 to 10 servings

ITALIAN CHEESECAKE

6 graham crackers, crushed to fine crumbs

2 tablespoons packed brown sugar

2 tablespoons unsalted butter, melted

2 packages (8 ounces *each*) cream cheese

1½ cups granulated sugar

1 container (15 ounces) ricotta cheese

2 cups sour cream

1 teaspoon vanilla

4 eggs

3 tablespoons all-purpose flour

3 tablespoons cornstarch

3 graham crackers, broken into 1-inch pieces (optional)

Fresh strawberries (optional)

Fresh mint (optional)

1. Line round 5-quart **CROCK-POT**® slow cooker with foil (see Note).

2. Combine crushed graham crackers and brown sugar in medium bowl. Stir in melted butter until crumbs hold shape when pinched. Pat firmly into **CROCK-POT**® slow cooker. Refrigerate until needed.

3. Beat cream cheese and granulated sugar in large bowl with electric mixer at medium speed until smooth. Add ricotta, sour cream and vanilla; beat until blended. Add eggs, one at a time, beating after each addition until well blended. Beat in flour and cornstarch. Pour filling into prepared crust. Cover; cook on LOW 3 to 4 hours or until cheesecake is nearly set.

4. Turn off heat. Remove lid; cover top of stoneware with clean kitchen towel and replace lid. Cool 1 hour. Remove stoneware from base; cool completely. Remove cheesecake to serving plate using foil as handle. Cover; refrigerate until serving. Garnish with graham cracker pieces, strawberries and mint.

Makes 16 servings

NOTE: Lining the interior with foil allows you to remove the entire cheesecake and cut it into traditional wedges for serving. To line **CROCK-POT®** slow cooker with foil, remove the stoneware from the base and place upside-down on work surface. Tear off a 24-inch–long piece of 18-inch-wide, heavy-duty foil. Place shiny-side down on top of upside-down stoneware. Smooth foil to stoneware, folding and tucking as necessary to fit. Remove foil, turn stoneware right-side up and place foil inside it. Smooth foil as much as possible to interior of stoneware, then lightly coat with nonstick cooking spray.

BANANAS FOSTER

12 bananas, cut into quarters
1 cup flaked coconut
1 cup dark corn syrup
⅔ cup butter, melted
¼ cup lemon juice
2 teaspoons grated lemon peel

2 teaspoons rum
1 teaspoon ground cinnamon
½ teaspoon salt
12 slices prepared pound cake
1 quart vanilla ice cream

1. Combine bananas and coconut in **CROCK-POT®** slow cooker. Combine corn syrup, butter, lemon juice, lemon peel, rum, cinnamon and salt in medium bowl; stir to blend. Pour over bananas.

2. Cover; cook on LOW 1 to 2 hours. To serve, arrange bananas on pound cake slices. Top with ice cream and warm sauce.

Makes 12 servings

INDEX

No-Fuss Macaroni and Cheese
Page 147

METRIC CONVERSION CHART

VOLUME MEASUREMENTS (dry)

1/8 teaspoon = 0.5 mL
1/4 teaspoon = 1 mL
1/2 teaspoon = 2 mL
3/4 teaspoon = 4 mL
1 teaspoon = 5 mL
1 tablespoon = 15 mL
2 tablespoons = 30 mL
1/4 cup = 60 mL
1/3 cup = 75 mL
1/2 cup = 125 mL
2/3 cup = 150 mL
3/4 cup = 175 mL
1 cup = 250 mL
2 cups = 1 pint = 500 mL
3 cups = 750 mL
4 cups = 1 quart = 1 L

VOLUME MEASUREMENTS (fluid)

1 fluid ounce (2 tablespoons) = 30 mL
4 fluid ounces (1/2 cup) = 125 mL
8 fluid ounces (1 cup) = 250 mL
12 fluid ounces (1 1/2 cups) = 375 mL
16 fluid ounces (2 cups) = 500 mL

WEIGHTS (mass)

1/2 ounce = 15 g
1 ounce = 30 g
3 ounces = 90 g
4 ounces = 120 g
8 ounces = 225 g
10 ounces = 285 g
12 ounces = 360 g
16 ounces = 1 pound = 450 g

DIMENSIONS

1/16 inch = 2 mm
1/8 inch = 3 mm
1/4 inch = 6 mm
1/2 inch = 1.5 cm
3/4 inch = 2 cm
1 inch = 2.5 cm

OVEN TEMPERATURES

250°F = 120°C
275°F = 140°C
300°F = 150°C
325°F = 160°C
350°F = 180°C
375°F = 190°C
400°F = 200°C
425°F = 220°C
450°F = 230°C

BAKING PAN SIZES

Utensil	Size in Inches/Quarts	Metric Volume	Size in Centimeters
Baking or Cake Pan (square or rectangular)	8×8×2	2 L	20×20×5
	9×9×2	2.5 L	23×23×5
	12×8×2	3 L	30×20×5
	13×9×2	3.5 L	33×23×5
Loaf Pan	8×4×3	1.5 L	20×10×7
	9×5×3	2 L	23×13×7
Round Layer Cake Pan	8×1½	1.2 L	20×4
	9×1½	1.5 L	23×4
Pie Plate	8×1¼	750 mL	20×3
	9×1¼	1 L	23×3
Baking Dish or Casserole	1 quart	1 L	—
	1½ quart	1.5 L	—
	2 quart	2 L	—